A FLY ON THE WATER

Also available from Allen & Unwin

NEW ILLUSTRATED DICTIONARY OF TROUT FLIES
John Roberts

THE FORGOTTEN SKILLS Country Crafts Remembered
Norman Mursell

A FUTURE FOR GAME?
Colin McKelvie
Foreword by H.R.H. The Duke of Edinburgh

BOATFISHING FOR TROUT
Steve Parton

SEASONS OF CHANGE
Rural Life in Victorian & Edwardian England
Sadie Ward

TROUT LOCHS OF SCOTLAND A Fisherman's Guide
Bruce Sandison

MY SMALL COUNTRY LIVING
Jeanine McMullen

COME DAWN, COME DUSK Fifty Years a Gamekeeper
Norman Mursell

THE CHANGING YEAR
Proteus of *The Field*

GREEN AND PLEASANT LAND A Countryman Remembers
Norman Mursell

FRANK SAWYER: MAN OF THE RIVERSIDE
Sidney Vines

DAYS AND NIGHTS OF GAME FISHING
W. B. Currie

NEW ANGLES ON SALMON FISHING
Philip Green

KEEPER OF THE STREAM
Frank Sawyer

EVER ROLLING STREAM
Bernard Aldrich
Foreword by H.R.H. The Prince of Wales

A FLY ON THE WATER

Conrad Voss Bark

Illustrated by Charles Jardine

London
ALLEN & UNWIN
Boston Wellington Sydney

George Allen & Unwin (Publishers) Ltd,
40 Museum Street, London WC1A 1LU, UK

George Allen & Unwin (Publishers) Ltd,
Park Lane, Hemel Hempstead, Herts HP2 4TE, UK

Allen & Unwin Inc.,
8 Winchester Place, Winchester, Mass 01890, USA

George Allen & Unwin Australia Pty Ltd,
8 Napier Street, North Sydney, NSW 2060, Australia

George Allen & Unwin with the Port Nicholson Press
60 Cambridge Terrace, Wellington, New Zealand

First published in 1986

ISBN 0-04-7990341

Set in 11½ on 13 point Plantin by Grove Graphics Limited, Tring, Herts.
and printed in Great Britain by Mackays of Chatham

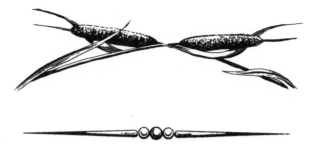

For Anne

Contents

Preface

THE fishing column of *The Times* appears once a week, or perhaps it is best to say that it is generally intended to appear once a week, mostly tucked away at the bottom of one of the sports pages, though occasionally it may be half way up the page and on some rare and notable occasions it may even appear at the top, and fame it is indeed to be lodged alongside reports from Twickenham or Old Trafford; but a lead story on fishing is rare; and on great sporting occasions, such as the Olympic Games, the fishing column is apt to disappear completely for several weeks, and only come back, as if on tolerance, when all the Gold Medallists have left, the flags are down, and the stadium is bare.

Preface

This is as it should be. As a former revered News Editor of *The Times* once observed: there is no news in fishing. He was quite right. The last news of any importance occurred some forty or fifty years ago with the discovery of the weighted nymph. Since then there have been some minor changes, worthy of a paragraph or so, but that is about all. It has therefore been extraordinarily kind, indeed altruistic, of *The Times* to have allowed me to ramble on about fishing for the past seven or eight years when they know, and I know, that nothing at all of any significance to fishing or to fishermen has occurred or could have occurred in that time. That, I think, is the mark of a great newspaper: that it allows its correspondents to ramble.

Here is a selection of rambles, some changed, some extended where an extension seemed to be justified, but many published for the first time. A word of warning is perhaps necessary. In a collection of essays written at different times in varying circumstances, consistency is not to be expected. Some of the stories are true, or as true as I have been able to make them, but are nevertheless offshoots of the imagination, creatures of mood to be dressed up, polished, and rehearsed, as on a stage, sometimes pointing a finger at human frailty or folly, sometimes and indeed more often gay and frivolous, sharing a joke with you, nudging an elbow, and certainly not to be taken all that seriously. If any philosophy appears to emerge there is little doubt it may have happened largely by accident.

I must thank so many people who have contributed, perhaps unconsciously, to these pages that I find it impossible to know where to start, for rarely have so many ideas been scavenged from so many sources, but some credits at least are given in the Notes and Explanations at the end of the book. My thanks are especially due to Norman Fox and his staff on *The Times* for their forbearance and encouragement, and to my wife Anne, the best fishing companion.

Conrad Voss Bark
Lifton, Devon, 1986

The passionate
fisherman

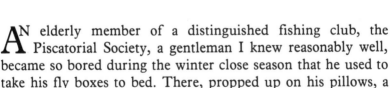

AN elderly member of a distinguished fishing club, the
Piscatorial Society, a gentleman I knew reasonably well,
became so bored during the winter close season that he used to
take his fly boxes to bed. There, propped up on his pillows, a
cup of hot chocolate or something of that kind on a bedside
table, he would open up his boxes of flies and fantasise about
their contents.

Night after night he would sit there, taking out his flies,
admiring them, smoothing them, no doubt discarding those that
displeased him, starting with his boxes of salmon flies, he had
three or four of those, and the next night concentrating on his

1

boxes of sea trout flies and thereafter on the following nights on more than half a dozen boxes of trout flies, spiders and nymphs, wet and dry, leaded and unleaded, until the time came round, possibly within a week or ten days, to begin again with the salmon. Thus engaged, he happily passed most of his winter evenings.

What his thoughts were, what idle dreams were evoked by such fingerings, it is impossible to say, for he never mentioned them, but most fishermen would hazard a not unreasonable guess. The sight of a well-tied fly is in itself a stimulus to the imagination and a box full a visionary feast in which our thoughts can drown in enchantment. So it must have been with him, until, sad to say, his wife began to complain about his habit, no doubt unconscious, of dropping flies on the bedclothes. These, no doubt accidental, discards became hooked up in the sheets and on several unfortunate occasions in her nightdresses. This was too much − she was not, you must understand, a fly fisher herself − and my poor friend was banished to a bedside chair, a dressing gown, and carpet slippers, if he wished to continue playing with what she contumaciously described as his toys. Being an agreeable man, as most fishermen are, he obeyed, though for some reason or other, which is difficult to explain, he found that sitting by the bed was not so satisfactory a stimulus to the imagination as sitting in it. His fantasies suffered.

Students of ethics, and I suppose ethics is still taught these days, will at once appreciate that this was a conflict not between the good and the bad, as conflicts are supposed to be, but between two opposing goods. The wife, plucking an errant Blue Charm from a sensitive part of her anatomy, possibly in the dead of night, had a legitimate complaint. The husband, unable to quell or diminish the number of his droppings, could either abandon his hobby, which was unthinkable, or pursue it in some safer place. It was the source of what might be called a moderate dissatisfaction.

The point of the story, as astute readers will already have recognised, is the professional attention given by the passionate fisherman to his craft, the sober assessment of the value of this fly or that, decisions that are taken in tranquillity, or which were taken in tranquillity before the trouble arose, to discard one pattern for another, to improve this one with a beard hackle, or a wrapped hackle, as the case might be, in preparation for what must be, at least in the imagination, a splendid season still to come.

Moreover, although we have been talking mainly about flies, my elderly member was assiduous in his attentions to other parts of his equipment, spending a great deal of time earlier in the evening in varnishing his rods, oiling his reels, cleaning his lines and all the other essentials of a fisherman's winter work, but of course his main pleasure, now denied, was to sit in bed, contemplate his flies and consider the prospects before him. Fortunately there was a happy ending. His wife, a good woman at heart, allowed him back into her bed, with his boxes, providing he counted his flies before and after.

GEORGE ORWELL, even in middle age, had what he called a peculiar feeling for fishing. As soon as you thought of fishing, he said, you thought of things that did not belong to the modern world. It was a tranquil occupation, belonging to his childhood, and to a world which he felt had vanished a long time ago, before aeroplanes and Hitler and the concentration camps. If he had been writing today he might have substituted riots, muggings, hijacks and the bomb. Each age has its burdens.

In spite of some legitimate exaggeration, Orwell was really saying that to go fishing is a way of escape. So it is, up to a point, for it makes a change and gets us away from the pressures of work, but is it something a little more than escape. A lesser-known writer but a greater fisherman, H. B. McCaskie, thought:

Escape is a poor word, with something of the Freudian jargon clinging to it; the Greeks had a nobler name for it, and called it ecstasy; a standing aside, a withdrawal from the common world.

3

I am not so sure about ecstasy either; certainly when one arrives at the river there is a feeling of tremendous excitement and anticipation, and it becomes vitally important not to waste a moment putting up the rod, threading the line through the rings, and tying on a fly. Of course, as like as not, we are so anxious to get everything ready that we bungle the knot, or the threading of the line, and when we get to the river we may well put the fly into a bush behind us or into a reed in front and even if we do get it on to the water it may well hit like a stone. If this is ecstasy it is not immediately recognisable as such.

We have, it is true, escaped or stood aside from the pressures of the common world but the world to which we have withdrawn is not all that empty of pressure; indeed there are times when it seems to be pretty full. Its frustrations may be of less importance than those of the market place but they are by no means without significance. A river has many ways of getting its own back on its uninvited guests. Humiliation of one kind or another is always likely round the next bend.

Escape may not be the complete answer, even though it must be a considerable part of the compulsions that lie behind the instinct to go fishing. Perhaps by chance we have stumbled on the right word, for the instinct to hunt goes well back beyond *homo erectus* and remembered time and is unlikely to have been dulled all that much by our comparatively recent civilisations.

There is, too, the possibility of other and more subtle influences, such as the fascination of water.

From early childhood most of us have been attracted to deep and silent pools and have stared into them, absorbed their mystery, and wondered how such unlikely creatures as fish can live in an environment so alien to ourselves. This is an approachable mystery, something that may even be not far away from the end of a garden, and delightfully one that can be touched and explored by the magic of rod and line. I can still remember, as a small boy, the heart-stopping excitement of a red-tipped quill float beginning to tremble on the surface of the water, suddenly going flat and sliding away, then coming upright, only to dip

4

fiercely below the surface. Oh, the astonishment and even terror as I felt the bottom of the pond move.

Perhaps one could say that we go fishing to return to our childhood pleasures, or to satisfy our atavistic instincts, or to stand aside from the immediacy of the world and to enter a more primitive and certainly a more beautiful existence, or perhaps all of these things in a mixture of emotions which we may dimly understand but are unlikely to be able to explain.

FISHING is not a game, declared an article in one of our sporting magazines, and one wondered, after a pause, why the writer thought it had been necessary to say so. There are, indeed, many occupations, quite apart from fishing, which are not games. War is by no means likely to be called a game and yet no one seems to object to Henry V's cry 'The game's afoot' before the charge at Harfleur. Indeed, now we have mentioned it, let us indulge the luxury of giving it more scope:

> I see you stand like greyhounds in the slips,
> Straining upon the start. The game's afoot:
> Follow your spirit; and, upon this charge,
> Cry – 'God for Harry! England and St George!

The words always bring tears to my eyes for they recall the time, the very first time, when I saw Laurence Olivier play Henry at the New Theatre just after the war and nearly came out of my seat with excitement. However, let us by all means return to fishing. The phrase 'fishing is not a game' is curiously emphatic, indeed, so far as I can remember, the word *game* is printed in italics as if the author was so incensed at the comparison that he wanted to condemn it out of hand. There is a whiff here of intolerance, of some undercurrent of emotion on which words, like icebergs, go deeper than appear upon the surface. If so, and at a guess, one might suspect the residue of a schoolboy's dislike, or even dread, of organised games, when it was imperative, however unpleasant, to turn out for the House XV, and the recollection of tremendous relief when the name was missing from the pinned-up list so that there was a possibility of escape by oneself to the nearest waterside. On that, of course, it is perfectly clear that fishing is nothing to do with a game.

Fishing, or at least the more primitive forms of fishing, has a comparative freedom from the restrictions, the rules and regulations, of organised games. Yes, indeed. There is no equivalent to the drop-out from the twenty-five, or perhaps one should now call it the twenty-two, and the only penalty kicks will be those we create ourselves from some blunder or other in handling our rod and line. All the same, rules and regulations about fishing have multiplied considerably since the halcyon freedoms of childhood. Alex Behrendt explains:

> Wherever a group of people live, work, or even play together, a certain code of behaviour must be established. The wildest savages have very strict tribal laws and anyone who breaks those laws is dealt with very effectively, with the result that all members of the tribe live well organised lives within the boundaries of their discipline. A good fishing club is fundamentally a hunting group, and the stricter the rules the better the fishing.

Strict rules, in some cases emphasised by strict though unwritten codes of behaviour, are now applied to most of our fisheries, overcrowded as they are or could be if there were to be free access to all. Fishing, especially fly fishing, may not be a game, in the sense of two opposing teams whose aim is to score off one against the other, but all the same it is without much doubt subject these days to considerable rules and restrictions which might be called, without too much stretch of the imagination, game laws.

The passionate fisherman

EVERY now and again someone comes up with the idea that in fly fishing, and this applies especially to trout, the fish themselves are of less importance than the art, or the craft, of fishing for them. That is not to say that the fish are not important. Of course not. As Arnold Gingrich once wrote, the fish are the star performers and if they weren't about there'd be no sense in fishing for them.

The point which I think he and others are making is that the art of putting a fly to a fish is in itself so satisfying and rewarding when one gets it right that this will keep you happy for a large part of the day, even if the crowning experience of the take is fairly limited or even non-existent. Contrary to Gingrich, I find this so as much if not more in salmon fishing than for trout. I once spent a whole day, that is to say a whole winter's day in the off season, learning under instruction to do a reasonably good Spey cast: not necessarily a good Spey but one that goes out a reasonable distance with a straight line and not a wiggly one. I had as much pleasure from this, and as much satisfaction at the end of it, as I would have had if I'd been fishing and had a fish. I came back home bouncing with pride, the same kind of pride that you get on a golf course when you've made some remarkably able approach shots. There is a pride in the skill. That seems to be the essence.

I once saw Lionel Sweet casting to salmon on the Usk with a spinning rod, an artificial minnow, and a centre-pin reel. He controlled the reel with the forefinger of his right hand and doing this he was able to check distance and avoid over-runs. Each cast the minnow went out and dropped a foot or so from the opposite bank, varying with the variations in the bank, dropping exactly where he wanted it to go. He didn't catch a salmon that day but somehow that did not matter all that much. It was a perfect demonstration of a superb skill which he enjoyed doing for its own sake. It gave him a considerable pleasure to be a master of his art.

For myself, I find spinning boring and not to be encouraged, but that did not prevent me acknowledging the skills of a man who can use a centre-pin with such accuracy. I am myself only interested in the fly. Over the years I must have shown some improvement in presentation though I am still inclined towards a too-wide loop and a poor roll cast, often without thinking, and no doubt other weaknesses, but that is something one lives with and puts up with, always promising yourself you will do better next time.

It is like any other skill, whether it's the knowledge of the Ruy Lopez opening in chess, how to hit a golf ball straight, or put spin on a tennis ball, the sheer pleasure of doing something difficult well. The fact that you are presenting a fly properly means, give or take the absurdities of fish and favour, that on the whole you may have a better chance of taking a salmon or a trout than if you did not present it well. Like most statements about fishing that needs to be qualified. One of the worst salmon casts I ever made, on the Somerley water of the Avon, produced one of my biggest salmon. A huge fish shouldered its way through a tangle of line, picked out the fly from the middle of the tangle, went down deep and fast and hooked itself.

But one should not deal with exceptional cases. There always are such cases. However much we may be a dilettante with a fly rod, however rarely we get to the water, however little we may care about our casting, there will always come a point, sooner or later, when we feel it could be much better than it is. Then, as with improving our swing at golf, we should go to a professional.

THERE are some fishermen, fortunately not many, who are so enthusiastic about their own particular subject, whatever it may be, that conversation with them, in the ordinary sense of the use of the word conversation, is impossible. After a little while one gives up trying to get a word in edgeways and merely listens, giving an occasional nod or a mumble of agreement. It is almost certainly dangerous to argue with them as they then become incensed at your stupidity in not understanding what they are saying, their voices rise higher, and they become even more emphatic and loquacious.

There are, as I say, not many fishermen of this kind, and those there are become fairly well known, sooner or later, and can with some tact and ingenuity be avoided; all the same, with some effort, they are often worth listening to providing one has arranged a safe escape route in advance. I had one such the other day in the club for half an hour lecturing me on a new system of fly casting which involved raising an elbow and saying at the same time something like 'high, flick, block' — or words like that — which would mean putting an extra couple of yards or so on your distance. We were all very kind, for there were several of us there, and said how marvellous and we must try it sometime and the party began to dissolve discreetly, except for one poor chap who was trapped in a corner and I believe was taken away to suffer further over lunch.

All the same, I do remember something that he said, which he may well have thought of little importance, but for some reason or other it has stuck in my memory even though it happened at least fifteen or possibly twenty years ago. He said that fishermen were inclined to enjoy all the activities which surrounded fishing as much as they enjoyed fishing itself. I think this is largely true and I was reminded of it because of the pleasure I had from tying what I thought was a remarkably good salmon fly. It was a Blue Charm on a single hook, a small one, and most of my previous Blue Charms had suffered from the disadvantage that the mallard wing was inclined to split, and the fibres to separate, thus giving the fly a rather spiky look instead of a neat smooth wing with the fibres as close together as on the original feather. This, of course, makes no difference to the effectiveness of the fly from the point of view of the salmon, only from mine.

And my point of view is the only one of which we have knowledge, for the salmon's remains remote and mysterious and not to be interpreted by man with any certainty. Those things which determine the effectiveness of the fly, as human beings are able to judge effectiveness, are much more likely to be

9

influenced by human values than by any others. Our judgments are accordingly limited to our perceptions of form and shape and colour which we ourselves find pleasing and which we hope, no more than hope, the salmon will find pleasing also. So far we can go, but no further. We tie what we think is a beautiful fly, or a fly which pleases our own aesthetic senses in the matter of colour and shape, neatness and size, and hope for the best. No man can do more.

Mr Walton and others

ZAAK WALTON, you may remember, was confused about milkmaids. Come to that, he was confused about many things, but let us deal with one confusion at a time. He imagined – or at least he gave us the impression that he imagined – that milkmaids had no cares, that they were happy, sang frequently for the delight of anglers, were chaste and virginal and clean, sleeping soundly at nights between lavender-smelling sheets.

Pure fiction; but what admirable fiction it turns out to be that can last three hundred years and go into four hundred editions world wide and still remain as young and fresh and readable as ever. The truth about *The Compleat Angler* is that it is not only admirable fiction, it is a picture of Arcady.

Walton wrote it first as an angling textbook and even after twenty years still thought of it in that way, though by then he had changed its original text almost beyond recognition. His final version – the fifth edition – was completed when he was an old man, his wife and most of his family and friends were dead, and he was looking back on many happy years. Without knowing it, he created a pastoral idyll which would capture men's hearts and minds for generations to come; creating a world that compensated for his loneliness.

And what a world it was – Maudlin and Coridon, milkmaids and shepherds, friendly inns and good companions, and through it all moves Walton himself as Piscator, dispensing friendliness, kindness, queer tales and a homespun wisdom of a quality and charm that has rarely been equalled. Some of the tales may be nonsense in one way, yet not in another, for there is something particularly attractive in the thought of pike being born from a pickerel weed – for is not pickerel a pike – and stranger things may have happened than the birth of flies from sun-warmed dew. One makes allowances for such irrelevances. It makes no difference to the charm of a fairy tale that one does not necessarily have to believe in fairies to enjoy it.

What is permanently enjoyable in Walton and has never been challenged is the quality of the man himself that comes shining through on almost every page, at times in almost every line. It is this as much as anything else that has given him immortality. You may try to define what it is, this elusive charm, but you will almost certainly be unsuccessful. The only thing to do is to give Walton his head and let him speak for himself, and one cannot do much better than to quote what he said of his intentions in the last passage he added to the fifth and final edition:

> I will walk the meadows by some gliding stream, and there contemplate the lilies that take no care, and those very many other various little living creatures that are not only created, but fed, man knows not how, by the goodness of the God of Nature, and therefore trust in him. This is my purpose; and so let everything that hath breath praise the Lord.

DAME JULIANA BERNERS was not confused about milk-maids. It is we who have been confused about her. We have thought about the Dame as the mother figure of angling, just as

Iszaak Walton has been regarded as the father figure, and we have thought of her for something like 500 years as the editor or compiler of the first English textbook on fishing, *The Treatysse of Fysshynge Wyth an Angle*, published in 1496.

Not so, according to Jack Heddon, fly fisherman, historian, antiquarian. The book was attributed to the Dame by mistake. It was said to have been published at St Albans in Hertfordshire. No. It was at St Alban's *House* in Westminster, part of William Caxton's press. Heddon made his discovery in the 1970s after years of research in the muniments room of Westminster Abbey. It was already known that Abbey historians had located the site of William Caxton's printing press close to a large building known as St Alban's House. This building filled most of the space covered by the green to the east of the Chapter House where today the statue of King George V stands. Heddon consulted the *Treatysse* and there, on the original text, was the printer's imprint, known as a colophon, giving the site where it was printed – *Apud villa sancti Albani*. Near St Alban's House, not St Albans city.

There was more evidence, but the conclusion was already clear. Dame Juliana Berners, Abbess of Sopwell near St Albans, was not the author of the *Treatysse*. The author was an unknown writer who added chapters on fishing to a book that already dealt with hunting and hawking, completing a gamefair book for the medieval gentry. Sadly we do not know the name of the author nor is it likely that the name will ever be discovered. Meanwhile we still think of Dame Juliana as our mother figure. She has been with us too long. There is nothing like a Dame.

Some of these early writers on fishing are not quite so remote from our own time as people may imagine. Who do you think it was who first urged anglers to be sure to keep farm gates closed after going through them and not to fish a river without permission from the owner of the water? No, not Walton. Way back beyond Walton: Dame Juliana Berners, the *Treatysse of Fysshynge*, 1496.

I like to stick to the idea of the Dame. She had a wry wit and a sharp tongue. She would have been pretty hot in condemning commercially sponsored competitions for money prizes. Listen to this. You can almost hear her saying it:

> Also, you must not use this aforesaid arteful sport for covetousness, merely for the increasing or saving of your money but mainly for your enjoyment and to procure the health of your body and more especially of your soul. For when you intend to go to your amusements in fishing, you will not want very many persons with you, who might hinder you in your pastime. And then you can serve God devoutly by saying your customary prayers. And in so doing you will eschew and avoid many vices, such as idleness, which is the principal cause inciting a man to many other vices, as is well known. Also, you must not be too greedy to catch your said game [*fish*] as in taking too much at one time, a thing that can easily happen if you do what this present Treatysse shows you. That could easily destroy your sport and other men's also. When you have a sufficient mess [*a dish, a catch*] you should covet no more at that time. Also you should busy yourself to nourish the game in everything that you can, and to destroy such things as are devourers of it. And all those who do according this rule will have the blessing of God and St Peter.

I am with the Dame all the way, or most, though I am not sure that I serve God devoutly by saying my customary prayers during a rise. They were more intimate with God in those days, though I do call on his name during times of stress.

A bit further on from Berners, or whoever it was wrote the *Treatysse*, you come to a pretty downright blustery sort of chap, one of the commanders in Cromwell's army, Colonel Robert Venables, who was the scourge of the Irish and altogether not the kind of a man who would be an amiable fishing companion at all. However, he wrote a very good fishing book, mostly about bait fishing but parts about the fly. In fact, one short passage in his *The Experienced Angler* is a superb description of the way to fish the fly:

... the fish will sometimes take the fly much better at the top of the water, and at another time a little better under the superficies of the water; and in this your own observation must be your constant and daily instructor, for if they will not rise to the top try them under ...

Now that seems to me to be pretty good. It is as modern as Goddard or Skues. Putting it another way, Venables is telling us that sometimes the trout will take the nymphs ascending to the surface to hatch and sometimes they will take the winged insect on the surface and you have to decide what is happening by observing the water.

Walton must have disliked Venables intensely, for Walton was a staunch Royalist, and Venables was very much a Puritan and a Parliament man, and as the civil war was going on at the time, or had just finished, I doubt they ever met, but Walton praised Venables' book, which I thought was pretty generous of the old man. Mind you, Venables was sound on coarse fishing, especially ground baiting:

In such places as you use to angle at, once a week at least, cast in all sorts of corn boiled soft, grains washed in blood, blood dried and cut into pieces, snails, worms chopped small, pieces of fowl or beasts' guts ...

Venables didn't spend much time on fly fishing, only two chapters out of ten, which is about average for the seventeenth century as most angling in those days was bait fishing, in midwater or 'on the ground', meaning ledgering. All the same you get hints from the way he writes that he had a certain affection and admiration for the fly and fished it as often as he could even when he was harrying the Irish. In fact that phrase of his about the trout sometimes taking the fly at the top of the water and sometimes a little under the superficies of the water has lasted much longer than he might have expected. It is *at the top of the water* that sticks in the mind. Did it mean a floating fly and if so how did he keep it afloat? It might be that he fished downstream, with the wind, allowing only the fly to dap on the surface. A horsehair line is very light and a dap is easy with an 18-ft rod. It can't have meant what we call a dry fly. Could it?

A stone memorial to G. E. M. Skues (1858–1949) was unveiled on the banks of the Abbots Barton water of the Itchen on August 9, 1980, near the place where his ashes were scattered by his friend, Mullins, the keeper.

Poor Mr Skues. He had a lonely life. A number of fishermen who ought to have known better were unkind to him. Eventually, he had to resign from the Abbots Barton water where he had fished for 56 years. His stretch of the Itchen has now become a place of pilgrimage.

George Edward Mackenzie Skues was a solicitor with an office in Essex Street, off the Strand. He was a bachelor, never seemed to have a lady friend and always lived alone. One of his favourite haunts, apart from the rivers, were the rooms of the Flyfishers' Club which were then in Swallow Street, off Piccadilly. He loved to sit in one of the leather armchairs there, stroking the club cat, talking fishing with his friends. Some disliked talking to him. He was an outcast to some of the members, a pariah, a man who believed in fishing the wet fly on dry-fly-only water. That, in Halford's time, was heresy, appalling bad manners, unsportsmanlike. Today, Skues' copies of fishing books from his library are among the club's most valued possessions. His memory is cherished, the heresies forgotten.

Skues, to look at, was a rather short, stubby man, with baggy clothes and thinning hair, and he had what he liked to call monocular vision. One eye did not work. With one eye, however, he saw more and understood more about rivercraft than most of his two-eyed contemporaries. He tied delicate and beautiful flies which are also treasured by the club. He was a jolly man with a nice sense of humour and he liked to be liked and he liked good company but he could be as stubborn as a horse when he was challenged, as he often was. Most of us can be when we know we are right.

Skues was originally a dry-fly-only man himself, a disciple of the great Halford, and he took Halford's word that the dry fly was the only possible or permissible method of fishing the chalk streams. All went well and he enjoyed himself and was one of the boys until one day he was fishing a dry fly to a trout which consistently refused it, until by chance the fly happened to sink in the surface film and the trout then took it. Why, Skues thought, should the trout take a sunk fly when the best of all possible methods was the floater? From that moment on the enquiries and the experiments began. The quest was started that was to last for forty years.

At first he was attracted to the idea of fishing the same types of wet flies that were traditional in the North and the Borders, but after he had used a marrow spoon – the first man to do so – to examine the contents of trouts' stomachs he changed his mind. Instead he tied patterns to imitate the creatures he found, mostly nymphs of the *Baetis* species, and in 1910 his book on nymph fishing, *Minor Tactics of the Chalkstream*, challenged all the assumptions of Halford and the dry fly purists.

In those days it was often thought that Skues was something of a bigot about fishing the nymph, but his writings make clear that the nymph to him was always a method ancillary to the dry fly, to be used as an addition to the dry fly man's technique, not as a separate method of fishing on its own. But such moderation – and indeed he was a fair and moderate man – was not acknowledged by his opponents at the time. He was not fixed in his views. His own nymphs were unweighted, but when a river keeper, Frank Sawyer, thought of weighting the nymphs to fish them deeper Skues gave him every encouragement and helped Sawyer with his writing. Gradually, but only very gradually, the idea of fishing the nymph on chalk streams gained ground, and

17

before he died Skues was comforted by the knowledge that he had made a major contribution to the fishing of our time.

THAT gifted fisherman, David Jacques, once wrote that the actual capture of a trout was insignificant compared with the absorbing experience leading up to it. There is much to be said for this, and also for the truth of the motto of The Flyfishers' Club – that there is more to fishing than catching fish. Arthur Ransome, teller of children's tales, who used to write on fishing in the *Guardian* newspaper, then the *Manchester Guardian*, in the 1920s, put it like this:

> Escaping to the Stone Age by the morning train from Manchester, the fisherman engages in an activity that allows him to shed the centuries as a dog shakes off water and to recapture not his own youth merely but the youth of the world.

Ransome found hyperbole necessary to express the depth of emotion, the inner tension, the anticipatory excitement of the angler setting out with rod and line into the unknown. A similar imagery – indeed in almost the same words – was Howard Marshall's, who said that to go fishing was to shake hands with the caveman. The experience was put, less vividly perhaps, by that pioneer aero engineer and scientist, J. W. Dunne:

> The appeal of a sport – being simply an appeal to age-old inherited instincts – is never experienced in its full perfection unless there is involved some call upon that craft of the wilderness, that faculty of appreciating the ways of bird and beast, and fish and insect, the acquirement of which was, through countless centuries, the one great, primary interest of primitive man.

Television is a fairly uneasy bedfellow as far as fishing is concerned. It tries hard. There is no doubt about that. The camera shows us men fishing, sometimes a number of men fishing, and some of them at least are seen catching fish, and are thereupon interviewed, their tackle and their baits discussed and all in very friendly terms with a helpful interviewer. It is most efficiently done and great efforts are made to convey to the viewer the interest and excitement that everybody involved must feel, and yet it all seems to fall flat.

It was restored, fortunately for us, in at least one programme in which Michael Hordern behaved as fishermen are known to behave and not as television producers hope they will. Hordern took the part of Arthur Ransome, following the same streams, wandering up river, slipping on rocks; the camera following like a pet dog, staring into his face, catching the glint of his eye, the expressions of the hunter. We saw him bungle his cast, get the hook caught in his woollen mittens, heard him mutter 'sod it' as his fly lodged in a bush.

It was no longer the fish that mattered. It was the man, the truth of man's experience captured in the beautifully spoken commentary in the words Ransome had used fifty years before:

> It is said that gardeners and fishermen make fine old men. This is not surprising. They have been caught up into nature,

grow old with a good will and no hanging back, and are without misgivings about their own mortality.

THE business of the poet, said Dr Johnson, is to interpret nature. No better way than with Ted Hughes, Poet Laureate and fisherman. Consider Hughes' description of the rise of a salmon:

> Then the pool lifted a travelling bulge
> And grabbed the tip of my heart nerve, and crashed . . .

The travelling bulge grabbing the tip of the heart nerve is a new insight into what happens when the fly goes over the fish and the fish rises. One sees it precisely and clearly and with a greater understanding of how we feel when it happens. The poet writes of ordinary experiences in ways which encompass a general truth, and explains to the reader or the listener emotions which may until then have been only half understood, if indeed they have been understood at all: the way that cormorants mutilate a pool, the damsel fly that hovers over the water in her snakeskin leotards, the gape of a salmon on the redds. He recreates for us with a brilliant imagery how a big fish crashes out of the water and leaves behind

> . . . a crater of suds.

He observes, notes and records with a clinical detachment the way of water in a stream, the riding whorls of water

> that loosen and melt
> into the bellies of pools.

The pike, he tells us, has a malevolent aged grin, and we see it. When a crane fly is blown on the water he tells us that its jointed bamboo fuselage has crashed. So it has. We have all of us talked of the blue flash of a kingfisher but he calls it a blue flare, which gives the real feel of speed. In a hundred ways he interprets the river and the river creatures. He is passionately involved, at the same time is a dispassionate observer.

Sometimes, indeed very often, the images that he uses are not immediately explicable in modern or practical terms but go back to the symbolism of the old gods. He describes the feelings of a man fishing for sea trout at night. Out in the dark fields, out in the corn

> . . . a horned god is
> Running and leaping
> With a bat in his drum.

A haggis and a whisky grog

AT one time during the First World War relations between the Allies were not all that good. It was decided that publicists from both countries should be exchanged to write nice things about each other in order to improve morale. A French publicist was sent to Balmoral to see King George V fishing. This is a literal translation of part of his report:

He is an angler of the first force, the King of Britain. Behold him there as he sits motionless under his umbrella, patiently regarding his many-coloured floats. How obstinately he contends with the elements! It is a summer day in Britain,

22

that is to say a day of sleet and fog and tempest. But, what would you? It is as they love it, those who follow the sport. Presently, the King's float begins to descend. My God! But how he strikes! That hook is implanted in the very bowels of the salmon. The King rises. He spurns aside his footstool. He strides strongly and swiftly towards the rear. In good time the salmon comes to approach himself to the bank. Aha! The King has cast aside his rod. He hurls himself flat on the ground on his victim. They splash and struggle in the icy water. Name of a dog! But it is a 'braw laddie'! The ghillie, a kind of outdoor domestic, administers the coup de grace with his pistol. The King cries with a very shrill voice 'Hip Hip Hurrah!' On these red letter days His Majesty King George dines on a haggis and a whisky grog. Like a true Scotsman, he wears only a kilt.

THE post-war generation was assured by all those who should have known best that when women were liberated they would be happy. It does not seem to have worked out that way. Indeed, to judge from what has been written about one of our leading feminists, Miss Germaine Greer, the liberated woman is now almost universally plunged in gloom. She believes, so we are told, that she lives in a sterile society, that governments are corrupt, that giving birth is painful, anaesthetics dangerous, fertility frightening, infertility shattering and contraceptives murderous.

It is a fairly formidable list and even if only part of it is true it is almost certainly a major reaason why so many men take up fishing. To spend an entire weekend with a misery bag of a companion who keeps on complaining about her body being a battleground of warring ideologies would become a little tedious, to say the least. One would need sooner or later to get away.

Not that men are immune from depressions. Not at all. Even

fishermen can become broody at times. There was the celebrated case of a former Provost of Eton who when he felt the black cloud coming over him would take a rod and line down to the Thames. He found fishing to be a cheerer of the spirit, a diverter of sadness, and a calmer of unquiet thoughts. Whether fishing could cope with Miss Greer's unquiet thoughts is another matter but it might be worth giving it a try.

The fact is that quite a few women, liberated or still in thrall, have taken up fishing in the past ten years or so. Whether this is to escape from turbid thoughts or simply that they like fishing is difficult to say. Perhaps a little of both. Certainly they find, as men have already found, that gloom cannot persist within sight of a rising trout and that sadness is successfully diverted by the take of a two-pounder.

It might be assumed from this that the neuroses of the liberated woman may be more contagious in cities than when exposed to the country air. Such things may be mere palliatives but if woman's despair at her destiny cannot be banished entirely it may still be modified, if only for a time, by a spell among the water meadows.

SAY a prayer for the soul of Negley Farson, an American reporter who lived hard and drank hard and wrote like an angel. Has anyone ever written a better description of what one sees when fishing the voes of Shetland:

> The softly waving seaweed forms a brown lace around the rocks of the voe. It waves to you, rising and sinking softly with the long Atlantic swells. The seas foam up white, and run back hastily with little whispering regurgitations, to lie

still, so that the white tracery of tiny bubbles fades away, and you look sheer down through blue-green depths to where the shelving black rocks disappear into submarine forests . . .

He was trained as a reporter, and words were his business, but not many reporters could observe so closely and communicate what they see so well as that. I have an affinity with Farson, for he fished the Devon rivers that I know, except when he was wandering in the Kalahari or the Caucasus or places like that, for he had the same sense of adventure, the same instinct of the explorer, as Peter Fleming had in sending news from Tartary. They are fairly few and far between, these intrepid characters who go off with a knapsack and a pipe of tobacco into the wilds, but all those newspapermen I have known who do have turned out to be fishermen as well, especially fly fishermen.

Whether carrying a fly rod is in itself a passport to a friendly greeting from otherwise hostile natives is arguable; but certainly fishing, as with farming, is one of man's basic preoccupations, and to declare oneself as a fisherman might help to subdue to some degree a good many barriers that face the traveller. Farson certainly found it so, except on one rather unfortunate occasion in the Caucasus. It was not long after the revolution had taken place and he was among the first western correspondents to penetrate to any depth in the new Soviet republics. He was in fairly wild and remote country, where fishing helped to provide much-needed food, and there he met a Cossack who was one of the new Soviet instructors in communism. Farson was fly fishing and the Cossack strongly disapproved. He regarded this form of fishing as capitalist. He told Farson 'only the worm can be trusted'.

Farson fished in most countries of the world but reserved his deeper affections for the Barle and the Exe and other streams that are born on Exmoor. His advice on how to fish these little rivers could not be bettered. It was all a question of where you put your fly as you waded upstream, casting a short line with flies like the Blue Upright, Hare's Ear, Pheasant Tail or Greenwell, and

25

you will fish all day with a cast so fine it looks like a strand of a brunette's hair.

A great cricketer of an earlier generation, C. B. Fry, captain of Sussex and of MCC, once said he thought it was just as difficult to make a good cast as it was to make a century against the Australians. Those who have had the misfortune never to have captained Sussex or the MCC might be forgiven for thinking that even a double Spey is not so difficult, and certainly not so hazardous, as standing up to an Australian fast bowler at Lord's. However, Mr Fry should know. He did both.

But there, one suspects, comparisons with cricket come to an end. Fly fishing is not a spectator sport; and, with only a few minor exceptions, would be boring if it were. There is nothing much to see except a man putting out a fly to largely invisible fish. Even for other fishermen it becomes fairly tedious to go on watching for longer than half an hour or so, for apart from undoing some tangled nylon or tying on a new fly, not a great deal seems to happen. True, the man may put his fly into a tree, which can cause a momentary interest, but the likelihood is that even if a fish does rise to him it is over so quickly that most likely we would have missed it.

Even fishermen's triumphs are hardly spectacular. Catching one fish is not all that different from catching another and a superb cast between two beds of ranunculus which avoids drag, which is no doubt pleasing to the man who does it, is not likely to arouse much enthusiasm in the gallery. Interest is likely to flag and once that happens not even the most apt of commentaries is going to revive it. Watching a man fishing, to put it frankly, is bound to become a bit of a bore.

Luckily this is how fishermen like it. Nothing is so off-putting, even if it is only a small boy peering over a bridge, as someone watching the delicate process of a fisherman addressing a fish. This, like other personal occupations, is something that

26

should be done in private. It is far too delicate a matter to be exposed to the common view. It would totally destroy a man's confidence to know that his skills, or the lack of them, were open to public assessment, and his incompetence the subject of public debate. Fortunately it is unlikely to happen. And to come back to Mr Fry's analogy, it is a great relief to any fly fisherman to know that whatever he does he will never have to face the humiliation of a long walk back to the pavilion after being bowled for a duck.

IF, many years ago, you fished for salmon in the Blanchdown run of the Tamar, the Somerley water of the Hampshire Avon, at Easter Elchies and Delfur on the Spey, and for the big trout of Leckford on the Test, then you may remember Dr Philip Neighbour. You certainly will if you were ever on beat three at Ibsley or watched one of Oliver Kite's television programmes. Philip Neighbour was a great fisherman. All this was long ago. He is now a wax model in Salisbury Museum.

It is difficult to tell you in a few hundred words how it all happened, and to be truthful about it, and about him too, for it is far too easy to distort the truth, as any reporter will tell you, and this I may be doing, though I think not.

Neighbour was a contemporary of Rupert Brooke at Cambridge, was a graduate of Sidney Sussex, and served in France and Flanders during the 1914–1918 war. Most of his generation died in that war and when he came back he found that he could not easily settle down in the consulting rooms he had taken in Harley Street. There is a period here I know little about but I think it was now, in the middle 1920s, that he began to fish the Test. Fly fishing took hold of him. He felt the call of it becoming stronger.

There was, at one point, a crisis. How much of it was due to the war is difficult to say. He gave up a promising and lucrative London practice to become a country doctor in the heart of nowhere. He took over an old surgery in a stable block, at Comilla House, at Amesbury. The surgery consisted of two old and dilapidated rooms that had probably been there unchanged since Victorian times. Most of his patients were farmers and farm workers and their families. Some were so poor they could not afford to pay. In that case he treated them for nothing. They brought him a chicken, eggs, or vegetables in payment.

He had that country practice for something like fifty years. The local people thought of him as a good doctor but something of an eccentric. He had harsh words for those who came to him with very little wrong. To those who were really ill he was kindness itself. They got used to his habit of closing the surgery from time to time and putting a notice in the window: gone fishing.

Philip Neighbour retired in the late 1970s and died at the age of 88 in 1982. The surgery was so out of date no one was willing to take it on. Someone said, quite rightly, that it was a museum piece. To a museum it went. There it is today in Salisbury Museum and there are the models of the patients in the waiting room and the doctor listening to a patient in the surgery. The rooms are just as they were in the 1920s, probably little changed from Victorian times. The doctor looks as though he is all ready to go fishing. He is wearing a tweed suit with plus fours. His salmon flies are on a shelf near by. I wondered as I looked: what would he have thought of becoming a fisherman in wax?

THE last man in England to have been bitten by Dr Johnson's parrot is said to be still alive though bedridden in Esher. This is not quite so surprising as it seems. The man is a fisherman, and fishermen and parrots share a quality of longevity above the common run of mankind.

Doubt will perhaps focus mainly on the parrot. It lived, when last seen, in the public bar of the Cheshire Cheese, off Fleet Street, a cantankerous bird of a considerable age. It bit most people who approached it. Mourned by a large company, Dr Johnson's parrot died of heart failure during the Blitz.

Dr Johnson's house is just up the alley from the Cheese so there could be a connection with the doctor, though the parrot would have to have been at least 158 years old, if not older, when it died. Johnsonians have searched Mrs Thrale and Boswell and whoever else they can search without coming across any reference to a parrot. A cat, yes, called Hodge, but no parrot. They have also failed to come up with the quotation, once attributed to Dr Johnson, that fly fishing might be a very pleasant amusement though float fishing was a worm at one end of the string and a fool at the other. However, all that is a digression. Let us leave the parrot as an open question and return to the fisherman.

It is true, I think, that fishermen as a whole are a fairly healthy breed, especially those who cast a fly over mountain and moorland streams. Any man who has walked through deep heather, climbed boulders, and waded white water must be reasonably fit and well to survive, moreover there are intangible benefits:

> Often after walking a mile or two on the way to the river, at a brisk pace, there comes upon one a feeling of fitness, of being made of nothing but health and strength so perfect that life need have no other end but to enjoy them. It is as though till that moment one had breathed with only a part of one's lungs, and as though now for the first time the whole lungs were filling with air.

That ought to keep one going for a reasonable length of time, well past the eighties with a bit of luck, and it is said, with what authority I do not know, that fishermen in Baluchistan make it to a hundred or more. Whatever may happen in Baluchistan, the belief is certainly world wide in the truth of the proverb, variously attributed to the Chinese, the Medes, and the Persians, among others, that hours spent fishing are not counted against

29

the normal span of life. In that case, the gentleman abed in Esher still has a way to go.

Angels on a pin

THE schoolmen of the University of Alexandria, so history
has it, spent a considerable portion of their blameless lives
arguing how many angels could stand on the point of a pin. No
doubt the conclusion, if ever reached, would be of theological
interest but whether of any practical use is another matter. One
is reminded of the schoolmen by recent arguments on the
definition of a fly.

The trouble is that the more one tries to define almost
anything the more confusing and difficult it seems to become.
It should be fairly easy to define a fly, a winged insect of the
order of *diptera, trichoptera*, and so on, but even the dictionary
gets a little worried because it points out that the word also
applies to butterflies and dragonflies and therefore − how
admirably put − is virtually equivalent to an insect. The
angler's fly, however, causes no problems. It is a fish hook, they
say, dressed in imitation of a fly.

What, one wonders, is a popper bug which is dressed in
imitation of a frog, a General Practitioner salmon fly which

31

imitates a prawn, or one of those large multi-coloured reservoir flies which imitate, possibly unintentionally, ornaments on ladies' hats. The more one goes on with this, the more we flounder, the more the possibility of definition recedes. Maybe we should get on better if we began at the other end of the line.

Starting with the rod is an improvement in the sense that anything which can be cast by the fly rod is a fly, or can be said to be a fly, but not always. That is the snag. Lead-headed jigs or nobblers can be cast by a fly rod, just, but have been banned in some fly fishing competitions. Fly spoons and rubber eels are banned and so are quill minnows, though other minnows made of plastic are not. All very far from a definition.

Even the top people's dry fly clubs and syndicates on the chalk streams are inclined to suffer from uncertainty. One dry fly club has ruled that weighted nymphs may not be fished on their waters but an unweighted nymph, fished in the surface film, is permissible as it is only slightly damp. A fly that is only slightly damp can be said to qualify as dry. It was a splendid and ingenious way to resolve the conflict that was breaking out on the club water but it does serve merely to confirm the truth of Humpty Dumpty's law:

When I use a word it means just what I choose it to mean, neither more nor less.

Take for a Trout, two Lob worms well scoured, cut them into two equal halves, put them on your Hook; this is an excellent Bait.

THUS spoke Izaak Walton in the days when angling was angling, when there were no licences, no rules, no limits and you fished a worm or a fly as you pleased, using the same rod and line for both. At some time or another the bait and the fly began to go their separate ways. I am not sure when it happened. The so-called 'father' of the dry fly, G. P. R. Pulman, was still fishing bait as well as fly in the 1840s. They were dapping live mayflies on the Test until around 1900 or so. The divorce between bait and fly is comparatively recent. Nowadays it is pretty absolute.

I am not sure whether it was because of reluctance to impale worms on a hook, whether fly fishing is more attractive than bait, or whether new developments in fly fishing tackle meant that we had command of a far greater range and depth of water than our ancestors. Perhaps something of all three. I feel the Scots might have had an influence on the English in concentrating exclusively on the fly − Border fly fishing was well established as long ago as the late 1700s − but when the English really got down to it there were no half measures. This is Halford:

> Those of us who will not in any circumstances cast [a fly] except over rising fish are sometimes called ultra-purists, and those who will occasionally try to tempt a fish in position but not actually rising are styled purists . . . I would urge that the first rule to be observed by every man who wishes to be deemed a dry fly fisher is to follow the example of these purists or ultra-purists.

By now we may well be getting to the stage, if we are not already there, when angling means bait fishing; so that when you talk of an angler you mean a bait fisherman, not a fly fisherman; but the whole thing is very confusing for when a salmon fisherman talks about bait fishing he doesn't only mean worm or prawn but artificial spinning baits as well. Fly fishermen themselves, one suspects, would welcome the discrimination between bait and fly and some I know feel strongly on the subject. Hence the remarks that one occasionally hears about drowning worms or fishing with hardware.

Demarcation lines between bait and fly have been firmly drawn on trout rivers for a good many years and bait is gradually being banned on most of the better salmon rivers, not without protest in some cases, so that the process takes time. On trout-stocked reservoirs bait was still being fished in the 1930s −

and spinning continued at Blagdon until 1945 – but there were restrictions on certain baits, such as maggots and ground-baiting with maggots on public water supply reservoirs, to the annoyance of the writer of an editorial in *The Fishing Gazette*:

Maggots do no more harm than worms or any other creatures that inhabit these reservoirs

Maybe. Maybe not. However, baits on reservoirs began to fade out, and so did spinning, largely though not entirely because of pressure from water company accountants who put their weight behind the idea of fly-only as an economy measure, in order to reduce the cost of restocking. The fly took fewer fish than bait or spinner. So they thought. For a time it was true but new tackle and new techniques tilted the pendulum back again.

The spinner became the minnow fly, the worm and the maggot became larva and pupae flies, and the new synthetics stretched the frontier of the fly seventy feet down and forty yards distant. Our fathers would have been surprised at what the new rods and lines could do that no fly rods had ever done before.

Meanwhile the river fishermen, or a good many of them, were relaxing the rigid doctrine of the purists and the ultra purists. The fly was the fly, there was no doubt about that, but somehow it had now to be accommodated to the nymph; and that was not easy. It needed a good deal of adjustment. The Piscatorial Society, a club of ingenious and admirable fly fishermen, found the right way round. It is worth quoting the relevant passage from their rule book:

The style of fishing required by the Fishing Regulations on these waters is dry fly and upstream nymph. There are two styles of nymph fishing on chalk streams; one usually attributed to G. E. M. Skues, the other to Frank Sawyer and Oliver Kite. Skues lightly dressed his nymphs with soft hackle and used quill, herl, floss silk or dubbing for bodies. He fished them upstream, without drag, and just under the surface. He advocated 15 hooks as the largest suitable for chalk stream fishing. His style was intended to be used for trout which can be seen to be feeding at or near the surface yet not taking the dun or its imitation. It is a dry fly style to which Horace Brown, President of the Society in the early 1920s gave the name 'slightly damp'. The society includes this style in the term 'dry fly' on the Avon, Lambourn and Wylye.

PUBLIC opinion pollsters, in the shape of elegant young ladies with clipboards and an engaging smile, have been following fishermen about in recent weeks and asking them what at least some might have thought were slightly embarrassing questions. It is not all that agreeable to be approached by a perfect stranger, however charming, who asks how much money you spend on fishing in a year, what reasons you have for going fishing, and whether your wife approves or disapproves. One can imagine fact and fiction fairly equally blended in some of the replies.

However, we now know, for we have the assurance of the polls to call upon, that quite a number of all households contain at least one angler, and that there are several millions of anglers, some of whom go sea fishing, some coarse fishing and some game fishing. Of those said to be game anglers, some also go coarse fishing, some go sea fishing, and some do both. Those who do all three must certainly find themselves fairly fully occupied. The thought conjures up a picture of members of the Houghton Club dashing down to Dungeness on a Saturday night after the cod, hareing along to the Kingston power station stretch of the Thames for a ledgered barbel on a Sunday, and taking Monday off from the office for a deck chair and a snooze at Bossington.

Where pollsters ventured, social scientists were not far behind in their examination of what they rather loftily described as the angling sub-culture. This academic study of anglers, as you might imagine, was on a very different level from that of the ladies with clipboards, for the scientists included an emeritus professor, a reader in neurobiology, a psychologist and a sociologist, among others, who were determined to investigate the angler and angling in depth. Their brief, so we are told, was to examine the social, economic, therapeutic, environmental and ethical aspects of the sport; and their study, they assured those of us who read their report, was very different in its style and approach from previous studies of the subject.

So, for that matter, are some of its conclusions, for the 150 pages of charts, graphs, statistics and histographs are fairly formidable to the lay mind. Some indeed, owing to our ignorance of science, lean towards the incomprehensible. Even so, a vague picture of the average fisherman, a kind of composite angler typical of the breed, ultimately does emerge. At first glance the average fisherman seems to be about average. True, his income is generally higher than average but that is about all.

Studied in depth by the scientists, however, he turns out to be not all that likeable a character. His home life, whether average or not, does not seem particularly attractive. He is inclined to neglect his wife and family. His fishing trips, which provide adventure, excitement, and mental relaxation are taken alone or with men friends, and neither his wife nor daughters are invited. Breaking off for the moment, one wonders whether his wife and daughters want to be invited but this we are not told. He does at least take his son fishing occasionally, but not often.

The ideas of sex-equality, domestic togetherness and family relaxation strike few chords in his breast; and even if he does play stump cricket with his nearest and dearest during the annual week at the seaside he has an inbuilt inclination to disappear without warning with a handline towards the end of the pier. Not altogether a likeable chap, think the social scientists, even though they admit that his wife may be pleased at the effect the sport has on his general demeanour. That of course does largely depend on whether he has had any sport. His general demeanour could be pretty poor if he hasn't.

The final judgment of the scientists is pretty clear, even though it is not expressed in quite that limpid English one might have expected from senior university dons. They say:

> *the current norms of the angling sub-culture seem to run contrary to broader social trends.*

That seems to be that, yet on the other hand, as Professor Joad once used to remark, it all depends what one means by broader social trends. If they are of the kind of broad, indeed very broad, social trends that we see most nights on the television, the average fisherman's current norm, however contrary, might well be something to admire.

I AM fortunate enough to have inherited a small book, *Devonshire Trout Fishing*, written by a country schoolmaster, Charles Rabley, and privately published by a stationers in Launceston at a date not given, but probably at some time around 1913. Like many a Victorian or Edwardian writer Mr Rabley was fond of hyperbole: a river is not a river to him but the trout's watery home, that kind of thing, which sometimes makes for irritating reading, and he doesn't mind boasting about the number of trout he can take compared with other fishermen, but, all this apart, his advice on how to fish small Devon rivers is splendid.

I like Mr Rabley and I wish I could have met him, for he could have resolved one of the most extraordinary puzzles about fly fishing which has been nagging at me ever since I read the book. He writes, he tells us, of wet fly fishing. He uses a ten-foot rod, fishes up stream and on his gut cast he has a point fly and a dropper. That, you would think, means standard wet fly fishing practice.

Rabley's flies, which are illustrated in the book and from the look of them have been tinted by someone, but not very well, are also fairly standard patterns for west country rivers. For cloudy days he has light-coloured flies, mostly hackled, including the blue upright and hare's flax; for sunny days darker flies, various palmers, a dark mackerel and hawthorn, and for evening or after dark a white moth and a coachman. All are thickly hackled. His coachman, to judge from the illustration, is more bushed than the dressing in use today.

Now comes the problem. He is, remember, a wet fly fisherman and wet fly has to us one particular meaning. It means – again, obviously to us – a fly which is under the surface of the water. A wet fly. A fly that is wet. But does it have the same meaning to Mr Rabley? That is the problem. Here is the evidence: and, so that there will be no doubt about it, let us quote what he says in full:

> Every animal indulges in some sort of recreation and why not fish? I have heard it suggested that trout, when playing, repeatedly dash the water over the floating fly in order to thoroughly saturate its wings, and then, before swallowing it, enjoy the sport of hunting their victim below the surface while it possess any movement. I must say I have strong belief in this theory because of catching so many fish foully hooked during this diversion.

Well, yes, all right, but what this suggests is that he fished a floating fly, that is a dry fly, and that trout splashed water at it so often that quite a number of them were foul hooked. But let us go on. There is more:

> When fishing in the Carey on a lovely June day I was completely baffled in all my efforts at success with the fly rod although many trout were sporting in a promising stickle. Having fished through it blank I sat down and watched the fun going on, and never remember seeing the fish leaping so high into the air. I started again at the bottom end of the same water, and allowing the flies to sink some little distance, drew them slowly from the opposite bank across the water towards and above me. After a few draws a tug was felt, and as the line was

38

already straight I held on, and hooked the first fish and landed it. Continuing, and without seeing my flies, I took seven trout, averaging above ¼ lb, in 'drawing' the same water the second time. Not content with this novelty, after a short interval I tried again and got two more. I have adopted with success the same plan on many occasions and now feel convinced that trout do feed freely below the surface on insects, and can be caught by the artificial fly by touch as well as by sight.

I am no expert on the subject but I have read Pulman and Stewart and cannot find in either any reference to animating the sunk fly. Perhaps there is somewhere, I may be wrong, but it does seem to me that this obscure Devon schoolmaster was anticipating the induced take of the sunk fly by some thirty or forty years.

VIRGINIA WOOLF wrote a charming essay on fishing after reading Waller Hill's *A Summer on the Test*. She thought that fishing was both a creative and inspiring occupation. Mind you, she was thinking of dry fly on one of the best of the chalk streams. Even so, women novelists, who are generally regarded as being concerned with personal relationships as a basis for their work, are not known for writing about fishing. One cannot readily imagine George Eliot taking a rod down to the Mill or Jane Austen reflecting on the possibility of stocking the Avon at Bath.

Not really, but in the case of Virginia Woolf she was writing at the beginning of the age of emancipation. The slow, persistent infiltration into men's worlds was gaining speed. It would seem natural to her, as to our contemporaries, that women should be able to go fly fishing, if they wished to do so, just as it would appear to be a considerable infringement of their liberty if they were not. They have weapons at their command – indeed they have – to establish their rights.

There is the delightful story about the Anglers Club of New York, a luncheon club near Wall Street, which has an all-male membership. The wives of the members, or some of them, felt incensed that they could not join their husbands so they formed a club of their own, the Women Flyfishers. They were so charming and they fished so well that they were inundated with invitations to fish the best and most exclusive water possible. When their husbands heard of it they asked if they could come along too. They were told that the invitations were for women only.

But the fun of the whole business revolves around the considerable problem of what a woman flyfisherman is to be called. A *woman fly fisherman* is hardly right and yet the English language is such that gender cannot easily be indicated by a single word. It is a shade derogatory to change a *flyfisherman* to a *fly fisherwoman* because of the echoes of the word *fishwife* which may attach to it. A *fly fisher* could be male or female and yet if she were to be made a *fly fisherene* or something of that kind it would seem to be discrimination in reverse. Possibly, if *mankind* covers men and women, *fisherman* might be made to do the same, in time no doubt, with some adjustments to our mental attitudes.

A more serious problem is that when a woman dry fly fisher is good, as many are, they are apt to be extremely good. It is often said that a delicate hand is needed for a good dry fly cast. I think this is true and what is delicate about it is a sense of rhythm and timing, a feeling in the hand that spreads to the arm and to the body, controlled by a particular sensitive and perceptive mind. The *corps de ballet* has it at Covent Garden, that perfect and delicate sense of timing and movement. Men do not have this quality to the same extent. They cannot take over the graceful movements of the *corps* in the third act of *Swan Lake* or the finesse of the *pas de trois* in the *Nutcracker*. They lack, not only the shape and form, but the final delicacy of the timing and the gentleness of control.

And the point about fishing the dry fly is that these characteristics of delicacy, timing, rhythm and control, are more important than any other if presentation of the fly is to be perfect. Therefore, and possibly unfortunately from the man's point of view, women who take up the dry fly start with an

40

inbuilt advantage. It is not great. It is subtle. It does not exist, rather the reverse, when using wet fly, such as the double Spey, but in the presentation of the dry fly a woman, if she wishes, can be supreme.

The serious problem is that a woman can become so good she is better than her husband. In that case a little diplomacy is a good thing. If she consistently catches more and better fish than he does she might consider the possibility of restoring domestic harmony, if needed, by releasing one or two occasionally and surreptitiously so as to even up the score.

A myth of flies

TRADITION in fly fishing is to be respected. But not unduly. We are creatures of habit, it is true, but that is no reason why habit should not occasionally be broken with some advantage. After all, if it is not broken by ourselves it is frequently broken for us by others. Take, if you will, the arrival, and one needs to point out that it was a completely unexpected arrival, of composite rods.

To me, cane rods had been as lovable as friends, which indeed they were, and the thought of discarding a cane rod for some other kind of rod was unthinkable. Nevertheless the unthinkable arrived, under the guise of carbon, graphite, boron, and so on, and one had only to handle a 15-ft salmon rod made from these space-age materials to realise that sooner or later the temptation would be upon us and could not be resisted.

Breaking with tradition comes in other, though perhaps less

spectacular ways. For years I was in the habit of keeping my flies in rigid segregation, the equivalent of a fly dresser's apartheid, in which salmon flies must never be put into a sea trout fly box, and on no account must dry flies be mixed with wet flies, or wet flies with nymphs, and certainly there must never be any doubt which box contained nymphs for the lake and which for the chalk streams. I forget how many boxes this meant I must carry but it was quite a few.

Not that my flies are now mixed, God forbid, but after reading *A Summer on the Test* by Waller Hills it did occur to me that my segregation was a shade severe. Hills, you may remember, was a great advocate of the use of the Orange Partridge on the chalk streams and the Orange Partridge is a Yorkshire wet fly. In the Hills doctrine it is used as one might use a Houghton Ruby or a Lunn's Particular as a spinner in the surface film. No reason why not, and very sensible of Hills, but it does mean my wet fly box now has to become a little ambidextrous.

Cross-fertilisation goes on between salmon and sea trout flies to an advantage of the salmon. The traditional salmon fly has dressings fixed by years of inheritance. The cheeks must be so, and the horns so, the hackle this and the wings that, and the overall effect is charming and must not be changed; but as we know from fishing, shall we say, some of the big sea-fed Irish loughs, a salmon will take a sea trout fly and a sea trout a salmon fly without a second thought. And a brown trout will take both.

Naturally one must keep a sense of proportion. It is clearly unacceptable to tie a sea trout Peter Ross on a 5/0 heavy salmon iron but it will be nicely in balance on a low water salmon hook of about size 8 or so. Other sea trout patterns that one can try for light summer salmon fishing include the Blue and Silver, the Mallard, Delphi, Bluebottle and the Bumbles, and whether they will take more or fewer salmon than the traditionals is impossible to say but they do have a clear advantage in the simplicity of tying compared with a Wilkinson or a Silver Doctor, and if one has faith in them they can be fished.

On the other hand, it would be sad if our traditionals, such as the delightfully named Thunder and Lightning, were to

43

disappear from our fly boxes for good. It would be nice to keep some of them, if only for old time's sake. Sentiment, however, is unlikely to prevail for long against the pressures of the hairwings and the tubes. Change will continue to take place irrespective of our wishes; and it is perhaps advisable to remind ourselves that the tackle we started fly fishing with a mere fifty years ago – greenheart and gut and silk – are now largely cherished in museums.

A PUBLICITY handout from a leading publisher on a new fishing book claims that among other virtues the book clears away the myths of angling folklore. The claim is rather surprising. Presumably we are supposed to give two cheers at the thought of myths being cleared away but it is doubtful. Indeed if there was anything that would put us off buying the book it would be the thought that some of our treasured illusions might be at risk. Mythology and fishing go together as amicably as eggs with bacon and to have one without the other would be to deprive life of a good deal of its savour.

Certainly no aspect of fly fishing is as enjoyable as those which have a good, firmly based and well established myth or two for company. We do not wish to believe otherwise than that an east wind will blow the fly out of the fish's moth, that thunder puts the fish down, that heavy rain, light rain, a poor light on the water, especially during the time of the full moon, are all to our disadvantage. It would be a sad day that restrained us shading our eyes, looking at the sky, the water, seeing whether cows are grazing with their heads to the wind, their backs to the wind, or lying down, and delivering a solemn and deeply considered opinion on the prospects before us. It may be the wrong opinion, but, no matter, because if it is we can always say there has been a sudden change in conditions since our arrival.

The mythology extends wider. It is rampant among ghillies and water keepers, especially Scottish ghillies. There are those who believe that fly hooks must never be sharp, and those who believe they must never be anything else; and those who believe that a small single is an infallible hooker of big salmon and those who will have nothing whatever to do with them, and as for the pattern of fly there are as many opinions as there are galaxies. Those who write books on fishing, or those who write the publicity for them, must be aware of a further hazard. It is all very well claiming to have swept away some of the myths of fishing but the process necessary to do so will certainly create some more.

IT is a curious sideline of defence policy that reservoir flies are now taken seriously by the armed forces of the North Atlantic Treaty Organisation. Troops who have to land on barren, inhospitable, enemy terrain, are provided with survival kits, neatly packaged to fit a uniform pocket. The kit contains line, hooks, split shot, and instructions on how to find worms and maggots and other suitable creatures for bait.

In case the search for bait proves useless — presumably in an area of permafrost — the NATO planners have also thoughtfully provided four artificial trout flies for use in such or similar emergencies. There is no fly rod, unfortunately, though troops must be presumed to have sufficient enterprise to cut a withy or two for themselves, if there are withies within reach, but there are instructions about letting the fly work in the stream. The flies themselves, however, turn out to be rather large, neatly dressed reservoir lures.

Contained in little sachets they consist of a Muddler, an Orange Muddler, a White Matuka and a Sweeney Todd. The selection is of interest in many ways. Espionage agents of foreign powers will probably take it as an exercise in misinformation as the Muddler suggests landings in America, the Matuka in New Zealand, and the Sweeney Todd is probably put in because of army defence exercises around Rutland Water. Any *Gebrots* who is worth a rouble can see through that kind of deception at a glance. What is possibly of more interest to students of defence strategy is how the NATO Council knows that barren, inhospitable enemy terrain will always contain a reasonable number of fishable reservoirs.

THE Army has always been fascinated by fishing. Eisenhower was no mean fisherman and Bedell Smith always used to carry his fly rods with him during the 1944–45 European campaign; though it was not Bedell Smith who had the famous confrontation with a Russian general. The story goes that when the demarcation lines had been drawn between the American and Russian forces in Europe, the artificial frontier lines across Germany went in one place on one side of a reasonably good fishing lake which was said to be full of trout. When things had settled down and the remaining Nazi forces had been rounded up, an American general decided that he would go fish this trout lake.

So the American general whistled up his jeep and went off for the day with his trout rods, driving through lovely unspoilt pinewoods, until he saw the lake ahead of him. Much to his annoyance he saw it was being fished by a Russian general who'd also taken the day off and sloped away on his own. The Russian had a few words of American but the American had nothing but a Russian phrase book, so communication was not easy. The Russian, however, was understood to say that the American was trespassing in the Soviet Zone, to which the American replied that the Soviet Zone was on the far side of the water and did not include the lake. They got out their maps and there was a good deal of jabbing and pointing, until the American had the idea that they redraw the frontier through the centre of the lake, which would give the American a couple of good bays and the Russian a slightly larger area, though one with a predominance of marsh and shallow. The Russian agreed – for he was a bait fisherman and had his eye on that part of the lake – so then and there they redrew the frontier on their respective maps, signed the alterations, drank some of the American's whisky, and began to fish in harmony and friendship. At the end of the day the American had a couple of nice trout on the fly and the Russian had a nice couple on the worm.

The splendid fishing didn't last. The first sign of the change was observation towers built in clearings made in the pinewoods and after that there were more and more armed patrols, and pioneer companies with barbed wire and stakes, and engineers with lorry loads of mines; eventually the lake was sealed off from both sides with mines and barbed wire and electrified fences. The American general came down one day with his staff and took a long look at it through binoculars. They saw the notice boards and the minefields and the men with machine guns on the observation towers and felt pretty sick. One of the staff turned to the General and asked, 'Why did they have to do all that?' 'Well,' said the General thoughtfully, 'I reckon they must have been expecting poachers.'

PROBABLY the most important thing about being a purist, certainly one of its main attractions, is knowing where you are. It gives any man a satisfied feeling to know where he is, just as it is a little anxious-making if he doesn't. The purist has no such anxieties. He always knows where he is. He also knows where other people are as well. All up and down the river there will be men fishing in exactly the same way as he is fishing, give or take a few minor variations which are encouraged and are within the rules, such as in the choice of fly, but even there the choice is within fairly narrow and agreed margins of size and colour and shape and texture. The restrictions imposed on himself and on others by the purist do in fact lead to a remarkable egalitarian method of fishing. Purists are all equal under the dry fly code.

This of course does lead to a certain amount of jibing from those who like the freedom of being able to fish as they want to, with rods and tackle of their choice, and flies of any kind and size and shape and colour that they please. To the purist, free fishing of this kind needs some form of restriction to be interesting enough to be enjoyed. It is true that trout can be taken in a number of ways, he will say, but for me I am only interested in taking them in a way which I find intellectually satisfying and emotionally stimulating, which is the way of the dry fly.

Within this rather restricted scope, of only fishing the fly on the surface of the water, there is more freedom than some would expect. There are, for example, something like twenty-nine different ways of tying a dry fly, which is certainly as many as the standard openings of most master games of chess. The twenty-nine openings ought to last even the most industrious of purists a season or two before they get bored. Then there is the vexed question of presentation and the avoidance of drag, and to be skilled in both would certainly take considerably longer than a final decision on the best of the twenty-nine varieties. Indeed there are fishermen with some fifty years' experience of the dry fly who would profess they need another fifty before becoming reasonably competent. To become as addict of the dry fly, one of them wrote, is to give way to

> . . . the most damnable lure the Devil ever invented to tempt the sons of Adam from their allotted toil.

SALMON flies are a nuisance. It seems to me, and possibly it may to quite a few other fishermen, that we have created far too many hooks and tubes and things on which they can be tied. It used to be very simple at one time. You had a hook, the heavier the deeper, and that was it. But no longer. We now have brass, aluminium and plastic tubes, and Waddingtons, and trebles and doubles and singles, and if I have counted correctly that makes a choice of seven holders for our dressings. It creates a certain amount of *angst* when faced with such a choice. The old enquiry − what fly do you put on? − is turned upside down before you begin, because it now becomes on what do you put your fly?

There is therefore a choice of seven hooks, and one is inclined to fluctuate abominably between them all, quite unable to decide which is best, swayed this way and that by advice from those who believe themselves, probably unjustifiably, to be more experienced and knowledgeable than ourselves.

I was at one time all for tubes, weighted or otherwise, partly because they were cheap and easy to tie and undoubtedly effective, but I eventually became rather bored with tubes and tried, for a brief period, a Waddington, but discarded that fairly soon as fiddly and difficult. I used Drury trebles for some time but I found I pricked my fingers too frequently in the tying; though a better reason for giving them up was the damage they caused to fish. After hooking a smolt on a treble which was fixed in both lower and upper jaw, there was no doubt what I had to do: I threw the rest of my Drury trebles away and have never gone back to them since.

That leaves the doubles and singles. I know that doubles are fashionable at the moment and singles are not, but all the same it would not take too much of a push to side me with singles; not the big meathooks of our grandfathers' time, for there is no need for them nowadays with our fast-sinking lines, and in any case they are bad hookers, but the reasonably sized singles that can take a medium mallard wing and still have something to clip off by the eye.

Talking of meathooks, I did once know a very fine fisherman

on the Tamar who used to swear by them, enormous things they were, big enough to take a small shark, and he would strip them in fast and watch the salmon chase them and when they took he would give a terrible bang to set the hook. That was how he'd fished for most of his life but eventually, after losing five salmon in succession, he tried something a bit less fierce and seemed to do as well if not better than before. No, I think meathooks ought to be museum pieces by now unless they are still in use in Norway where they seem to take fish in waterfalls.

So, for myself, I have gone over at the moment to small and medium singles. They seem to me to balance the dressing, a traditional mixed wing shall we say, to a degree of excellence that one does not see even on a good double. They should be housed in a clip box so you can see them properly and the hook points honed to needle sharpness, for a sharp hook is good and a blunt one is bad, and that is all that should be said about hooks. For the moment, until I change my mind, singles for most of the summer and brass tubes for the floods. Until I change my mind.

The taking place

SALMON fishing, someone once remarked, is the art of casting a fly to a fish which is not there. Some truth in that, no doubt, and yet, once in while, the inexplicable happens; not only is the fish there but it takes. There are as many explanations why it should do so as there are prophecies, but none carry more than a momentary conviction. We have to resign ourselves to the fact, repeated *ad nauseam* in most of the best fishing books, that salmon are unpredictable.

Having accepted that, we should be able to approach the river in what the ancients called a state of grace. Purged of false hopes, we can cast our flies where we will, enjoying the bend of the rod and the flow of the line for their own sakes rather from what may ultimately happen. There is ever hope.

There is always an underlying sense of expectation, sometimes acute, sometimes less acute, but always there, at the back of the mind, and when that dies and drifts away and the mind becomes blank and tired it is best to stop fishing. A rest is indicated, perhaps to put the rod on one side, perhaps to stop fishing altogether, for unless fishing is giving pleasure and satisfaction and that inner warmth of anticipation, it is best to leave it for another day. Fly fishing is not a business.

This is why I find some books on salmon fishing not entirely to my taste, mainly because they seem to insist so much on a professional approach, if one can call it that, the need to work hard, change the fly, back up, change the fly again, concentrate on putting the fly over the lie twenty or thirty times, and if that doesn't work change to a worm or a prawn or a spinner. This is all excellent advice, no doubt, but there is something about it which is not entirely agreeable. I do not want to be a professional in the sense in which I am urged to be a professional, I do not want to work hard, and concentrate hard and fish hard and keep on changing my fly or going over to a worm or a spinner. I prefer to keep to a fly, though I have been known to change the pattern from time to time; but certainly the thought of putting on a worm or a prawn, as one is bid, instead of a fly, I find, for some inexplicable reason, distasteful. If a salmon will not take my Blue Charm or my Torrish, I say good luck to it and wave it on its way in the hope that the next entrant to the pool may be in a better mood.

Naturally I would like to be reasonably efficient, and there is nothing wrong about being professional in putting out a line in the best possible way, making a double Spey look good as well as reaching out to a satisfactory distance, and in that sense one does work hard, but − and this is where I part company with some of our textbooks − there is, or there should be, a limit to endeavour. I would crave permission, one might say, to be something of a dilettante from time to time, when the mood takes me.

In fact, and one admits this with a certain reluctance, I have been known to burst into song while wading hip-deep in the middle of the Spey for no other reason than that I suddenly felt like singing. This is not the stuff of which good salmon fishermen are made; it would upset one's rhythm of casting and quite possibly upset the fish. The textbooks, or those I have read, never imagine one is so foolish as to bellow out Siegfried's song, or something that approximates to it, during the serious business of catching fish, but to the aesthete or the dilettante or whatever grouping I come under it is of considerable importance to be able to do so. Indeed, it is more than an aspect of salmon fishing, it *is* salmon fishing, a part of the experience.

Salmon fishing, I would suggest, is too frequently overlaid by theory. One book will tell you one thing, another one another. You must strike off the reel, you must keep a loop of line in your free hand, you must *not* keep a loop of line in your free hand, you must have a slack line, you must have a tight line, you must keep your rod point high, you must keep it low, if a salmon takes let him pull line directly from the reel, allow four turns of the reel before striking, always keep a loop of line hanging from the rod and when a salmon takes, wait until the loop of line is pulled completely through the rod rings before striking, do not have a loose loop of line, and so on.

One of the wisest fishermen of our generation once wrote something to the effect that when you had caught five hundred salmon you felt you knew all about salmon fishing, when you had caught fifteen hundred you began to have doubts, and when you had caught several thousand you were quite certain you knew little or nothing about it. And another salmon fisherman with great experience emphasised over and over again to me that one should approach a salmon river with a due sense of humility. 'We know nothing,' he would say. 'Nothing.'

There is, of course, an area of experience, limited no doubt, varying from river to river, almost from pool to pool, where advice can be of help, especially from a ghillie who knows his job, or from a fisherman who has fished it for many years. The places where salmon are inclined to lie will be known, and some of them will be famous as 'the taking place', and the flies that are most likely to take a fish will be known also. Nothing, however, especially any rigid doctrines about flies and tackle, should be taken as gospel.

How splendid though, with all this uncertainty, these conflicts, such multiplicity of belief, such violence of opinion, so many contradictory views, how splendid when things go right, and when, against all odds, we do precisely the right thing, make the right cast with the right fly, and feel a sudden heavy weight as if we are snagged into a log, then feel the log move. The fish surfaces, turning over silver, and then goes down to play deep and run the line out to the backing. An unforgettable experience.

SPORTING journals, valuable though they are, indispensable though they may be, are inclined at times to be over-influenced by size. True, it is always interesting to be told of the capture of a large wild fish by some fortunate fisherman, and we would like to see a photograph of it no doubt, in spite of the fact that illustrations of fishermen and their trophies do tend towards a depressing similarity. A man and a dead fish are not among the more attractive subjects for creative photography.

What makes it even more depressing these days is the fact that the breeding of jumbo-sized trout has become something of a business, so that record fish can be produced almost at will, if not out of a hat then certainly out of a stew pond. Our editors, poor men, are therefore forced to go on publishing week by week, month by month, year by year, more and more pictures of even bigger and bigger and − let us face it − uglier and uglier corpses. Once having started, it is a little difficult to know where it all may end.

Genuine record fish, as distinct from the artificial variety, are fortunately not all that frequent and do not give our picture editors the same trouble. Indeed, they may feel the lack of them, for a couple of generations at least have gone by since the last record salmon made the news – the 64-pounder taken on the Glendelvine water of the Tay in 1922 by the ghillie's daughter, Miss G. W. Ballantine. In the photograph taken of Miss Ballantine and her fish at the time, the poor girl looks a little stunned by it all, as well she might, for it was no mean achievement to take and play such a monster; and indeed another girl, Miss Doreen Davy, who took a 59½-lb fish from the Wye in 1923 so impressed a number of male readers of *The Fishing Gazette* with her abilities that she had offers of marriage as a result, which she tactfully refused.

There are, of course, legendary monsters. It is said that a salmon of 103 lb was taken by the nets in the River Devon near Stirling in 1902, possibly 1903, and an 84-pounder by the Tay nets in 1869, and if there is any likelihood of anything like that happening again, I think it is towards the Tay we should look, for it is a river with a justifiable reputation for very big and powerful fish.

There are other legendary monsters too, a 38-lb sea trout said to have been taken from the Tees in the early 1800s by a Mr Teasdale and a brown trout of 39½-lb taken from Loch Awe in 1866 by a Mr. W. Muir, who foul-hooked it and played it for 2½ hours before it was landed. One longs to have more details but, alas, they are lacking. Perhaps somewhere, mouldering away in an ancient attic, in some long-forgotten leather-bound fishing book, in faded ink on faded pages, is the true story of these great moments, recorded in full and splendid prose to sway posterity.

For most of us there is only a pretty slim chance of getting a record fish of any kind, unless one dips into a fish farm pond, and one cannot help feeling that is not quite in the same league as Miss Ballantine and Miss Davy. It is, I suppose, for those who like it, but if one wants really to work for a record there is apparently nothing like a carp. For a carp you have to camp out all night, night after night, for weeks, maybe months, for time is no object, and you sit in a waterproof tent night after night by the side of mysterious ponds together with your collection of highly specialised tackle, bottled-gas stove and tins of baked beans, and if you are very persistent and lucky you may get a carp of over 51 lb, which would be the British all-comers record. Funny about carp. The Germans eat them, the Chinese make pets of them, and the English catch them, weigh them, photograph them, and put them back again to grow bigger.

QUITE a few salmon fishermen, wading deep in fast water in a big river, have known the sudden spasm of fear as their foot slips and they lose their balance. Until that moment you have been in control, but then suddenly the river has you, you plunge, struggle, arms waving to help regain balance, aware of the inhuman power of the current, and then suddenly all is over and you are again in command. Mostly it will happen like that. Not always.

The Dart claims a heart a year is an old Devon saying, but the big fast Scottish rivers are even more dangerous. If a river does take you out of your depth, the main thing is not to try and swim, but to get on your back, head up, feet downstream, paddling to keep yourself afloat and keeping your mouth shut. If you do not panic and shout and struggle there will be sufficient air in you and your clothes to keep you afloat until you drift somewhere within reach of land.

A more likely danger, while we are on the subject of danger, is to get a hook in your finger over the barb. Providing it is a single hook and not too large it can be got out painlessly by a companion with a piece of string. The secret is in the piece of string. When the hook goes in, the flesh closes round the barb and the hook cannot be pulled out without using considerable force and inflicting a good deal of pain. The traditional way was to push the hook in even further, exposing the point and barb, cutting those off with pliers, and then the hook could be pulled back and out. Not advised. One can go to a doctor, of course, but that would mean losing precious hours of fishing time.

We come back to the companion and the string. The trick is to release the grip of the barb on the flesh by deepening the channel in the flesh made by the hook when it entered. This is done by pressing on the top of the hook shank. This pressure forces the lower part of the hook deeper into the flesh, thereby widening the channel it made when it entered. This in turn releases the grip of the barb. The deeper the channel the easier it comes out. Your companion holds a loop of string round the bend of the hook, you press down on top of the shank of the hook, very hard, and when you have pressed hard enough you shout 'Pull!' and he or she yanks on the string and out comes the hook. If you press down hard enough and the pull comes at the right moment, all you feel is a slight pluck.

While on the subject of danger, avoid sticky mud. I knew a man once, wearing knee boots, who stepped on a patch of mud, went in only to his ankles on both feet, but couldn't pull himself out. We had to pull him out of his boots and the boots had to be left behind. There is another kind of mud which is like quicksand. I know a patch like this on the Itchen which is known as Poachers' Corner and is said to contain the bones of many men. Not far away from there a contractor left a bulldozer on the bank and when he came for it the next morning there was nothing there but a large crater full of mud and water.

But hooks are the main hazard. Avoid using a heavy hook with a light rod, for the hook will sag on the cast and will be out of control. If a hook snags on the opposite bank and you have to pull to break, turn your back in case the hook comes away, for if it does it may be travelling towards you at something like a hundred miles an hour. There are many ways in which you can get into trouble with hooks. Someone I knew dropped a treble on the bathroom carpet in the fishing hotel where he and his wife were staying. His wife went into the bathroom with bare feet and hooked herself on the treble which was hooked into the carpet. What she said to her husband is not to be told.

ONCE upon a time my wife and I booked a gardener's cottage for a holiday on the Findhorn, and a splendid holiday it was, but when we got there we found that the gardener's cottage had had to be repaired, so the factor very kindly, and at no extra charge, put us into the big house instead. It was officially called the lodge, so I suppose there must have been an even bigger big house somewhere else, but this was big enough for us. It had twenty bedrooms.

It was an eerie experience for the two of us to be alone in a huge place this size, for the impression it gave was that it was waiting and needing a huge house party to fill these vast empty spaces with laughter and warmth and excitement, great crowds of pretty women and sporting men, whereas we more or less crept about, probing here and there, and talking in hushed voices.

We found the relics of house parties, cut deeply by knife into the shutters of one of the five sitting rooms. The dukes and earls and baronets had their names cut there alongside the dates on which they had hunted and fished, and taken so many salmon and sea trout, so many stags shot, so many grouse. A game book on wood. The dates were from 1880 to 1890. One felt sad. What had happened to all these people?

So passed the glories of the Victorian house parties, leaving the rooms empty, the beds stripped, the peat fires unlit, and the kitchens bare. We cooked our bacon and eggs like trespassers in a kitchen big enough to have fed a banquet at the Savoy, and we hung our rods in a rod room that gave us the impression it was large enough to house one of the armouries from the Tower. We did our best to enjoy ourselves. But time past hung heavily.

It would be wrong, however, to think that the big jovial house parties of the Victorian era no longer exist, they must if one is to judge from a recent advertisement in one of the handouts offering fishing which come from a famous London estate agency. This one advertises a fishing lodge to let in Wester Ross which has seventeen bedrooms. That gives sufficient scope for a big party of the old type. The final sentence puts it in no doubt:

Most tenants bring up their own cook.

The trouble these days of course is that most of us do not have our own cooks. It does rather limit the catchment area of the tenancy, for a rota of reluctant wives would hardly be acceptable to the laird, who from the advertisement clearly wants the thing to be done in style, even if it were acceptable to the wives, which again is unlikely. A lady from the Cordon Bleu would undoubtedly fit the bill if she were not too expensive and could be prised away from her haunts among the London counting houses and merchant banks.

One foresees difficulties, but unless we are going to accept that we are disenfranchised completely from having our big house party in Wester Ross in the style in which it is commended, there might be a way round. It might be possible to make do by hiring a mini-van and packing it full of convenience food of a superior quality, such as Fortnum's game pies, and things of that kind, canned potatoes and canned lobster soup, which can be eaten cold or heated without too much difficulty.

In anticipation, at least, there would be nothing so exhilarating as the thought of a house party of friends and relations, happy fishermen and their wives and girl friends, setting out for the far north up the beckoning motorway in a convoy of cars, with the mini-van and its load of convenience foods bringing up the rear. The whole splendid house party would be inspired with the same kind of excitement that has sent greater expeditions over far horizons, the exhilaration at the thought of a house party that will survive a fortnight in the wilds of Wester Ross without the cook.

Blue Charm

THE Tweed is very grand and spacious, indeed you might
say it is an aristocratic river. It abounds with castles and
keeps and impecunious noblemen who live in enormous piles of
masonry which are largely unheated in winter but look
impressive on their smooth green bluffs overlooking the river,
keeping up appearances, hoping for the best, struggling with
taxation and depreciation, sometimes against their will having to
sell a picture or so to keep going. That hurts a good deal but they
put a brave face on it and the river brings in a bit. Sometimes
quite a bit.

One day, perhaps, there will be no more paintings to go to
Christie's or Sotheby's and dry rot will have got an unrelenting
hold; new methods and new men will be taking over the river
and the great house will have to be sold for a hospital or the
headquarters of a multi-national, the farms will be bought, the

61

grazing let, the iron railings will come down and the old order and the lords of the land will have come down with them. The river has seen much change ever since the days when the ice went, and the bear and the mammoth came down to the shallows to drink, and it will see more, as indeed it is seeing now, for the water level is lower than it was, and the water is not so pure, and more young fingerlings die, and more of the big fish are killed before ever they get to their mating run.

Sitting on a rock in the early summer sun, waiting for the boat to take me over to fish the pool on the other side, I could see the great house in front of me behind a screen of trees, a beautiful house, long and elegant, almost the size of a palace. Turning my head a little I could look behind me and see the steep green hill and the few broken stones which were all that remained of the great castle of the moss troopers of a bygone age.

But then the boat arrived, and I was jerked back to the immediacy of the present. The water was low, the flow gentle, the river shallow, so that with a floating line one barely needed the standard length of nylon and quite a small fly would certainly be enough. The ghillie – and one should always take the advice of the ghillie – chose one that was even smaller, a Blue Charm single.

The fly went out about twenty yards or so and began to swing gently in the current, flickering now and again from side to side in the cross flows from submerged rocks. You do not work the fly on the Tweed as you are supposed to do on the Tamar. You let the current take it and play with it. Up it goes, down again, here to one side, then to the other, gliding, twisting and turning, a free flying creature of the stream, unhindered and alive. For the fisherman there is something hypnotic about the steady progress of the line downstream, something rather splendid in the way it glides and moves over the water, a perfect rhythmical movement.

Looking up at the hill of the moss troopers I saw with half an eye the faint draw of the line as it came round in a curve at the end of the cast, and tightened into it, and felt the fish. On reflection, I am not at all sure I can remember what I did to hook the fish, not being one of your experts who always strikes off the reel, or has a loose loop of line ready to let go so the fish is hooked in the scissors, or is not, but it does not seem to matter all that much.

Further up was a pool where the river narrows and the water goes fast over a lip of rock, and with increasing speed, but there is a nice back eddy just here, and somewhere between the fast flow and the eddy there is a place where salmon may rest on the bed of waters, perfectly in balance where the eddy meets the fast flow, though it is difficult for anyone who does not know the river to imagine such a place under the turmoil of white water. However, there it is, and the ghillies know, and they instruct you to put your fly just there, and hold it, letting it flicker, twining and inter-twining in the current, jigging and darting, and if the salmon are there they find it difficult to refuse. We had two in a quarter of an hour and then no more for the day. That is as it should be. Modera-tion in salmon fishing is now more essential than ever before.

I must confess to a marked weakness for fishing for salmon with a floating line and small flies during the late spring and summer waters, when the sun is warm and you can be in thin clothing, maybe even fishing in shirt sleeves. I once went up to a Highland river in March when the snow melt was coming down and in spite of taking fish I did not feel that I was enjoying myself as I had expected. Worse would be to go for the opening of the season in January or February. On a Highland moor with the wind coming straight from the Arctic, snowing hard, with ice on the margins, it could be unpleasant.

Six dedicated fishermen who tried it one year, going up on the night sleeper from Euston, found it worse than unpleasant. It was the bitter winter of '47. In spite of precautions, three of the party developed frostbitten hands and had to be taken to hospital. The fourth slipped on the icy rocks and broke his legs, so the ambulance came for him and took him to the same ward as his friends. The fifth fell in, nearly drowned, and had to be treated for hypothermia. The sixth was the only one to take a fish but he was so excited he had a heart attack and had to go in with the others.

Mind you, we're better equipped for cold water fishing than our ancestors, for the great salmon fisherman, William Scrope, fished the Tweed without waders when he was there in the 1840s. He left good advice on how to do it. 'Never wade deeper than the fifth button of your waistcoat. Look at your legs from time to time and if they turn purple or black it is advisable to consider leaving the water for a while to restore the circulation.' They were tough in those days.

THE best ghost I ever saw was on the Tay at Grandtully. I had gone salmon fishing at about three in the morning and the night was just about right for a ghost. A whistling wind, whispering grasses, a long dark lane with things that moved in the undergrowth and a pale gibbous moon riding the dark racing clouds. Surprising how primitive fears can be roused by a few rustles in the dark in wild country.

I was alone, not a soul for miles, and it was a long walk from the car to the river. The rustling seemed to get worse. More than once I looked back over my shoulder to see what was behind. Only the dancing shadows. Branches, waving in the wind, looked like skeleton fingers.

I felt better when I got to the river. I went over the last grassy rise and on to the gravel bank and there was something white in the middle of the river that moved up and down. It was in the shape of a man and the moving part of him was the rise and fall of an arm, but the thing that alarmed me most of all was that the man had no head.

You read of people being rooted to the spot, which is no bad description, for I felt myself go rigid, and cold, and for quite a time I doubt if I moved an inch. I kept on looking but the thing did not change from the first impression I had of it: a white shape without a head. Eventually I felt I had to do something. I waded out in the shallows towards the thing and when I got within a reasonable distance I said, very loudly, 'Good morning'. I felt rather a fool saying it, for it did not seem quite the right way to address a ghost, but the words merely came into my mind and so I said them. I was not prepared for the response.

'There's nae guid aboot it,' said an angry Scottish voice. 'I've been here all nicht and I've no had a fush. A hell of a morning and ye're here far too early for the saumon!'

He was a sea trout fisherman but whether he was poaching or not, or what the arrangements were about night fishing for sea trout and day fishing for salmon, I was in no mood to ask. He grumbled at me for a moment and then walked off downstream and disappeared into the mist. I could see why I thought he had no head. He was wearing a black sou'wester which was invisible against the shadows.

THERE are many stories about the Spey. The one I like best is about the distillery tanker and the iron bridge. I daresay the story must have been elaborated over the years, for it has been told from one fisherman to the next, time out of mind, but all the same, like most legendary stories, it must have been based on a great and notable happening.

On one side of the river there is a famous distillery, which produces a wonderful blend of superb whisky, and on the other side of the river there are places where they put it into store to mature. They take the whisky from one side to the other in a great tanker and the tanker crosses the river by an iron bridge, and the characteristic of this particular bridge, which makes the tale, is the iron railings. Topping the railings on either side are long iron girders which jut out over the roadway.

One day, so the story goes, a great tanker filled to the brim on its regular journey across the river took the bend of the road a bit sharp and the edge of the iron girder on the parapet ripped the tanker open from stem to stern. Half a tanker load of pure spirit fell out on to the bridge and into the river beneath, a famous pool it was, and the salmon in it began leaping about like mad things, poisoned and dead drunk, and some were so drunk that they leapt out on to the grassy bank, and stayed there, helpless, blind to the wide. No one, I was told, had ever seen a drunk salmon before, but they did that day, many of them, for the run had been good and the bridge pool was a fine holding place.

The poor driver of the tanker, thinking to salvage something from the disaster, went down the footway from the bridge and picked up a couple of fish which he came back with and put on the passenger seat of his cab. Then he went off to telephone. You would have thought that the police, when they arrived, would have had some sympathy for the poor driver, but no, they had none. They took the fish from his cab and booked him for poaching as well as driving without due care.

The thing I remember about the Spey, and this particular part of the Spey, is the beauty of it all, and the people who were there, and are perhaps there no longer, and one of them in particular, a great salmon fisherman, who, as Walton said, is now with God. I learnt more from watching that man fish for a few minutes than you could pick up in a couple of years, for he had a special gift of concentration allied with a technique that was wonderful to see. With him you had an immediate sense, a feeling of confidence, that he would be the man to take a fish when all others would fail. He had a great ability to cast a long line. That was one of the secrets, but by no means all. He knew where to put his line, and how it should be arranged so that the fly fished as it should be fished.

He always fished the fly. He was not particularly dogmatic about it, it was merely an attitude of mind, a personal preference. It was the way he liked to fish. He'd got to the stage where − I think this is true − he simply disliked fishing in any other way. A spinner was a fairly boring way of fishing and the worm was unpleasant and not to be encouraged. He disliked fishermen, and especially some rather popular fishing writers, who laid down rules about how to fish. People who had preconceived ideas about how to fish for salmon were, to him, of no importance. He would say, and it is worth quoting:

66

I still find myself bewildered on strange waters. I find myself sometimes humiliated by them. When you come to a river, take nothing for granted. Beware of dogma, of ideas you have obtained from other people who may never have fished this particular river at all. All rivers, all pools in rivers, are different. You must look and think and learn from the immediate experience of this particular river, and from the experience of others on this river. Above all, you must be humble and keep an open mind.

Oddly enough, the flies he used were scrappy little things which he tied himself, by no means elegant, certainly not the kind of flies that you would approve if you saw them in a shop. You wouldn't buy his flies. You would want something neater, more graceful, and more fully dressed. His were skimpy little things, a shrimp fly on quite small doubles with no more than a couple of golden pheasant feathers on it, or a dark hairwing, a bit bigger perhaps, but with very little hair, black with a spot of colour in the fibres and a wisp of a hackle. A Stoat's Tail or a Munro would be about the same, though they would have to be very fine, for he thought all commercial tyings were too heavy and overdressed. He would shrug his shoulders and say:

That's how it is. People like them like that. If you dress them too thin they think they're not getting value for money.

When he was fishing you could see him thinking the whole time. He was concentrating. He would never give up. Even when his heart was bad, and it became bad, he had that ability. He was never casual about fishing. He was always intent on it, always watching the line and the water. He would always say that you had to read the water. I think that was one reason why he was able to take fish when others couldn't.

I was passing him one day, going upstream to fish down behind him, and by chance saw a slight hump in the water near where he was fishing. To me it meant little or nothing, a swirl of the current but no more, but to him it meant something quite

different. He could visualise a fish, moving a little from the fast
flow to a slower, lifted by the current, the back of him bulbing
the surface. I did not know this at the time. He told me later.
What I saw, uncomprehending, was a sudden explosive reaction
on his part. Instead of fishing out the cast, he lifted the line and
cast above and beyond where he had seen the fish move,
accurately enough to bring the fly over the fish in the right place
and at the right speed. I saw the line tighten and the rod bend.
It was when you saw him doing something of that calibre that
you realised his mastery. Yet always he was humble. Always he
would say:

There is so much to learn.

IT may sound odd to most of us, but there are times in salmon
fishing when the number of fish that can be caught becomes
an embarrassment. There was the case not long ago of the
fisherman, a great conservationist, who declared that two fish in
a day were ample for any man. He was invited to fish the Tweed.
There was a prolific autumn run and he killed thirteen fish in
a day. They were photographed, and the picture published in
the magazines, whereupon he felt that some explanation might
be due. It sounded apologetic but it also sounded reasonable.
He'd had, he said, six blank days previously so he thought that
thirteen fish on the seventh day pretty well averaged things out.

Rod and line fisherman are not, on the whole, inclined to limit
their catch, though on the Grimersta, I think it was, someone
who took 35 salmon in a day returned 12 of them unharmed to
the water because he felt he was being a little excessive. There
was another man on the Tweed some years back who took 22
fish in an afternoon but then stopped fishing because he felt
he had caught enough. He might also have had in mind that
he and the ghillie would have to carry something like two

hundredweight of fish back home, and home might have been a long way off.

He could, of course – not knowing him I find it difficult to say – but he could have been one of those fishermen who have signed letters to *The Times* urging the protection of an endangered species; and, if that were so, to catch 22 of the species in an afternoon might have seemed a little unfortunate. He could hardly, in all conscience, go on urging others to limit their kill if his own would need the estate Land Rover to carry it away. Perhaps he could convince himself that in the excitement of the moment – and the afternoon must have been exceptionally exciting – he had forgotten his principles, but as soon as he realised what he was doing he stopped, and swore, no doubt truthfully, that it would never happen again.

Traumas of this kind must happen not all that infrequently to conservationist letter writers to *The Times*, especially if they happen to be good fishermen on prime beats. They are unlikely to have the stern self-discipline of the New York lawyer who is on record as having caught 32 salmon in a week, of which he kept only two. 'The first salmon,' he says, 'is the most difficult to release but after that you don't mind letting the next one go so much, and after a while you enjoy seeing them glide away upstream after you've taken out the hook.'

It is perhaps unfair to bring the Americans into it if only because our system is one of private ownership, while their rivers belong to the people at large and are controlled and regulated for the people by the various state departments of fishery and game. Some rivers, where the run has been poor, are closed entirely for fishing for a season or even longer, others have rigid controls, some are for fly fishing only, most have strict catch limits and for a fisherman to be found with more than the number of permitted fish with him means a heavy fine. Some fish and game departments have the power, as in Alaska, to close down fishing on rivers and lakes at a day's notice if they have evidence that the runs of fish are less than they should be. Anglers in Alaska have always to check with one of the 23 local offices in various towns to see what the latest regulations are in the river they want to fish. In most of the Alaskan rivers, which teem with salmon, no angler is permitted to kill more than two salmon in a day, the only exception is for grizzly bears.

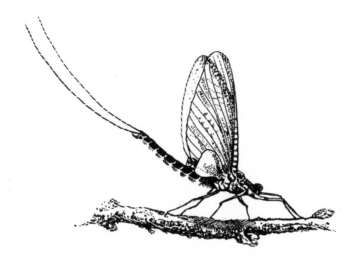

Bosky woods

HOW does one describe rivers? How does one describe the joy and pleasure of going fishing? We seem to fluctuate from time to time between the extremes of the romantic and the scientific and each age also has its own literary conventions. Some last and some do not. Especially do I find some of the late Victorian writing about rivers and the countryside a little tedious. This, for example:

> . . . the stream which goes purling through bosky woods and sylvan dells delights the angler . . .

Words like 'bosky' and 'sylvan' go out of fashion. The approach of the writers of nature notes is strictly more factual but has its problems.

Feather-footed through the splashy fen passes the questing vole . . .

That is a take-off but could be the real thing. Then there is artistic writing:

I went down to the river today and it was cold. The willow twigs and young branches were more orange, the ash had swollen, dark purplish buds. A flock of lapwings went over. A patch of butterbur is in flower.

The scientific approach is largely unreadable by the layman but lends tone to any article and is especially interesting for its unusual enthusiasms, especially those of the angler-entomologist:

there are the pale thin medium size longhorns (Oecetis spp), the large marbled *Glyphoteaelius pellucidus*, the various black silverhorns, and the rare and most beautiful *Chimarrha marginata*, with black wings edged with bright gold. My joy on capturing one of the latter some years ago on the R. Test was indescribable.

The indescribable joy of seeing a *Chimarrha* is something that most of us would applaud without necessarily being able to share, or possibly wanting to, but a river, even the R. Test, caters for all, as one remembers as a schoolboy, wading the shallows with bare feet, socks in pocket, shoes hung by their laces round the neck, turning over stones and watching for bullheads to dart away. The best of fishing writing captures something of that mood. Like this:

Fishing is so much more than merely catching fish. It is, by the clear waters of the Lambourn, an involvement in the life cycle of insect and fish, a participation in the organic growth of everything in the valley. From the caddis to the sedge, from the darting nymph to the emerging may-fly, everything is part of a living pattern in which the angler participates.

That gets well under the skin of what one feels about a river, and even if one does not feel it in quite that way it is by no means a bad start. The more one looks at it, the more one might come round to that point of view. It is in any case better than writing of sylvan dells and bosky woods.

THE dales and the wolds are mixed in memory, great open green hills, folded and contoured and smooth, cropped by sheep, the fields divided by dry stone walls that creep and wriggle up to the horizon. What you remember of these great uplands is a feeling of space, of greater stretches of sky and the blowing clouds that come racing over in a great hurry to get somewhere. You remember the harebells, the limestone outcrops, the cry of the curlew, and the sound of the wind and running water.

Somewhere here, when I was a schoolboy, I came across a man fishing. I wish I could remember now where it was for I would like to go back to it sometime and fish it myself. It was close to a market town somewhere in the East Riding, there was a bridge, and a little river, and it seemed an idyllic place for a man to fish, and I envied him.

He had a wicker creel on his back and a long rod – I now know it was greenheart – and he was wading upstream flicking the rod here and there in front of him, lifting the rod as the flies touched the water, letting them flow down for a moment, then casting again. I could see that his flies searched every foot of water in front of him before he took another step upstream and another cast. The rod was never still, the flies thrown forward, a slow lift as they drifted down, a lift off and another throw, this time a little to the left or to the right of where the flies had been before. Sometimes he would cast several times to a likely place, an eddy behind stones, a curl of water at the side of a faster flow, a sheltered pool close up under an overhanging bank.

I was watching from the parapet of the bridge and to begin with he was fairly close to me so that I could see he had one or two or possibly more flies on his cast, wispy little things they were, hardly visible. The line he had out was quite short, not more than about twice the length of his rod, and he never lengthened line at all as he went upstream.

I was fascinated. I'd never seen anything like it before, it was so rhythmic and delicate, and I suppose he had hardly gone a few yards upstream when the line tightened and a small trout came skittering to him over the surface of the water. He knocked it on the head and put it in his creel and went on. From that one small stretch of river he must have had four or five fish, one or two far bigger than you might expect to see in a beck that size, which was full of little rocks and swirling pools and racing water so clear you could see the coloured pebbles on the bottom.

I didn't know it at the time but I had been watching the most perfect demonstration of upstream wet fly fishing that one could possibly wish to see. I doubt if I have ever seen a better. That is why, when many years later I was fishing in southern England, I could never quite appreciate the remarks of some of my companions to the effect that the wet fly was purely a matter of chuck-and-chance it. Not if you have seen it fished as I have seen it fished, for then it is clearly and visibly a great and delicate perfection.

A spell of bright sun and a warmth in the air around March or April will bring out the first of the olives, not many perhaps, just the occasional fly coming off the water. In Devon it might be the March Brown, which are a little bigger than the spring olive, and a little darker, less bluey-coloured, but not easy to identify at a distance unless you are an entomologist.

Even earlier we might have seen a few iron blues, as I did once on the Tamar in early March. The river was high and coloured, a great rushing torrent of water coming through a narrow gut below a croy at great speed and there were the iron blues, a whole flotilla of iron blues, riding the tumbling waters of the eddy at the side of the flow. Not a trout moved to them, not a single fish, and there were these nice little dark flies, iron blues, no doubt about it from the colour and the way they held their wings, standing on the water like proud people enjoying the ride and the fresh air after being under the water for so long. It must be nice for them to have a complete new existence after being bugs in the mud and stones with nothing much to look at, unless it's weed and even weed could be a bit boring if you were stuck there staring at it for month after month. I may be slightly anthropomorphic, but is there not a case for thinking that when the nymph hatches into the winged fly, bursts into the light of day for the first time, and feels the power of its wings over the water, it might also feel something akin to what we regard as happiness?

One hopes so, but one does not know. Whatever is the case of the emotions of a fly there is no doubt about our own. It is all part of the processes of spring, of burgeoning birth, that starts in the hedgerows at the end of January, with little white speckles of snowdrops, then primroses and wild daffodils, and even though trout are well down and the water high and coloured there is a feeling that something is about to happen very soon.

One never quite knows when. One day we were up on Dartmoor in early March; it was bitterly cold, though the sun was out. There was no sign of fly or fish. The Dart was clear and had that nice peaty colour but not a thing moved. We wandered upstream and as we did so the sun went in, heavy clouds rolled up, darker and darker, until the mid-day light was almost like dusk, and then lightning flashed and thunder rolled but, surprisingly enough, there was no rain. Then, suddenly, without any warning, while all this was going on, the river came alive. The fly hatched and fish rose.

We took a trout each on an olive within the same ten minutes, fishing no more than twenty or thirty yards apart, and then the rise and the hatch ended and so did the lightning and the thunder and all was over for the day. No more fish. No more fly. The sun came out and all was tranquil and peaceful and quiet. That was our spring festival. There had never been one like it before, there has never been one like it since.

It is to remind us, if we need reminding, that the river has no rules.

RAISE your hat to Mr Leonard West who published a book a long time ago – I think in 1913 – in which he emphasised the importance of the midge. They were ubiquitous

in the high mountain becks or tarns, on the water meadows, by the reservoir or lake, or wherever trout or other fish are to be caught . . . On a calm summer evening a Gnat [*he called them gnats rather than midges*] on an 00 hook [*Redditch scale,* 16] will often do great execution when a more heavily dressed fly will meet with but scanty notice . . . and I may fairly say that Gnats have often succeeded in taking shy highly-educated fish when other lures failed; and they have turned up trumps when for a time at least the success or failure of an expedition was in the balance.

You couldn't say fairer than that. West tied about fifteen

different midge patterns, most of them with wings, and very pretty too they were, and he also had a nice pattern of the Daddy in various sizes. But to come back to the midge. His main colours were olive, black, green, ruby and brown.

Following on West we have had many patterns of midge, mostly of the pupae, splendid tyings by Dr Bell, J. R. Harris, C. F. Walker, John Goddard, and others. Many of the pupae are now weighted, so that they sink easily and can be fished at all levels, but I think it was Richard Walker's pattern which was intended to be fished in the surface film. Bell's Blagdon Buzzer was unweighted but as it was fished with two other flies on the cast, would sink fairly well. There are times when the emerger midge, practically dry, slightly damp, suspended in the surface film, is extraordinarily deadly. The first time I discovered this was − as so often happens − by accident.

I suppose West would have called it a mountain tarn, anyway it was a lake in the French Alps, quite small, well stocked and well keepered, a private fishery with day tickets, where most of the fishing was done by the local inhabitants using live grasshoppers on bubble float rigs which they cast out towards the centre of the lake from fixed-spool reels.

I had arrived with a fly rod and felt a little embarrassed by the sight of echelons of Frenchmen with bubble floats along the bank, shoulder to shoulder, and I had to push through a crowd of small boys all offering live grasshoppers to me at so many francs for one, a reduction for three. '*Mouche, mouche,*' I said, making various gestures, and they looked extraordinarily puzzled and shook their heads. Grasshoppers, yes, *Mouche,* no!

By chance, and of course such things occur only once in a lifetime, among the bubble floats out in the centre there was a good rise of trout, not to the grasshoppers but to some small dark fly on the surface. It was a heavy hatch of what I guessed was midge.

What I had intended to fish was a wet fly, a small Black Spider round about 14 or 16, pretty small, and intended to simulate a midge pupa. I was greasing my leader, got tangled up with something or other, and found that I had greased the fly, a Black

77

Spider, as well. Never mind. Finding a place for a back cast, which was not all that easy as the grass behind me was full of small boys hunting grasshoppers, I managed to get out a reasonable length of line and put the fly not far from the bubble floats and rising fish. I doubt if the fly had been on the water more than a few seconds before it was taken. In about three-quarters of an hour I had eleven fish and then I stopped fishing because I had enough. The greased Black Spider, a dry midge, had beaten the grasshopper brigade hollow through no virtue of mine, merely that I had been lucky enough to fish the right fly at the right time in the right place. I found myself surrounded by interested Frenchmen, none of whom had a word of English, wanting to know what I had caught my trout on. They could see it was a fly rod I had been using − most of them had not seen a fly rod in use before − but what was the *mouche*? I showed them, wondering for a moment whether the small boys would start hunting in the grasses for black spiders in preference to grasshoppers when I said it was an *araigneé noire*. My accent was quite appalling but they seemed to understand. I repeated *chironomid* several times and waved my fingers to show the flight of the fly and they said *araigneé chironomid noire* and looked pleased and slapped me on the back and said a great many things in rapid French about *les Anglais* and their *cannes*, which I took to be complimentary. I distributed my remaining stock of Black Spiders among my new friends, bought some of the small boys ice creams, and departed in a haze of goodwill and *entente cordiale*.

Relations with fish

WHEN I was a small boy I had a goldfish in a bowl which used to swim round and round and round in circles, which was really the only way it could go, for it was a very small glass bowl, and sometimes the fish would circle it in one direction and sometimes in the other; the only variety being to come to the surface and eat ants' eggs which I used to feed him, irregularly, when I remembered to do so. He died fairly young and so did his successor, who I brought home from a fairground in a plastic bag.

Our relations with fish — fish of any kind — are not good. I must confess that since my early goldfish days I find the sight of fish in an aquarium slightly depressing. I feel they ought to be free. They look depressed, hopeless and bored. Even if they have not experienced freedom, one feels they might like it.

It was not until I visited a fish farm that I learned that there must be some truth in this, as trout, in overcrowded conditions, develop neuroses. Crammed together in concrete tanks, fin to

79

fin, they suffer stress which may well be the cause of unbalance and other strange physical effects. The same thing is apparently happening to battery hens.

Genetic engineers have now produced, so we are told, a sexless rainbow which is said to be an advantage as, unpreoccupied with sex, they keep condition and remain a bright silver all the year round compared with the males who become dark and frustrated when unable to breed. Most of our rivers and all our still waters may by now be fairly full of unfulfilled, unsatisfied sexless trout.

To be honest, rainbows do not seem to have adapted happily to the English environment. In all but about five of our rivers – the Derbyshire Wye is one of them – the rainbows cannot produce self-supporting populations and in most of our lakes and reservoirs refuse to breed at all. They were, in fact, only imported to Britain from America in the 1880s because accountants had discovered they could be produced by fish farmers twenty per cent cheaper than brown trout. Mating takes place by hand-stripping the eggs and sperm into tin buckets. Does it, one wonders, give the rainbow the same pleasure as an orgasm on the redds?

Maybe our generation is becoming more interested in relations between man and fish. Scientists have been asking whether fish feel pain when they are hooked and fly fishermen have been taking up barbless hooks so as to cause less damage to the fish if they need to be released. I well remember one peculiar experience with a barbless hook.

I was on a Devon stream, fishing a Partridge and Orange into a lovely run of fast water just below a riffle on a bend, when I was taken by a very large brown trout, large that is for a Devon brook, because he must have been well over a pound. I brought him in to the slack water at my feet, and he was tired and became quiet, so I took the nylon in my hand, slid my fingers down to the fish's mouth, and tweaked out the hook. He knew at once he was free and turned in a flash, but then he stopped. Now the surprising thing happened. I can see it still. He turned about, came back to my fingers which were still in the water, appeared to look at them closely, turned away and vanished.

He was a very lovely trout, beautifully coloured, a perfect specimen in the finest of health, which was why, on impulse, I gave him his freedom; but what bewildered me was the way he returned to examine the fingers that had freed him from the encumbrance of the hook. Possibly one puts it down to curiosity − these pink things in the water must have been strange, especially when they moved − and fish are intensely curious creatures; yet, on the other hand − no, really quite impossible − nevertheless the thought persisted. Could it have been gratitude?

I THINK it is true that we are more concerned about the suffering of wild creatures than we were. In my grandfather's time it was fairly common to rip out a hook and chuck the trout on the floorboards of the boat − they always fished the drift − and leave it to suffocate in the air. Today we are more inclined to kill a trout quickly and mercifully with a blow on the head to shorten its suffering, that is indeed if we want to kill a trout at all. There is a move, especially on those rivers where the wild brown trout is still the main inhabitant, to take only fish we need to have for the larder and release those we do not.

There is also a move to discover how and to what extent fish feel pain, which is something that does not seem to have concerned fishermen until the last few decades or so, and there is a further move towards the use of barbless hooks to facilitate the unhooking of trout we do not wish to keep.

Curiously enough, the use of a barbless hook does not seem to have any effect on the number of fish that are brought to the net. Without the barb the hook appears to set deeper, is not normally dislodged by leaps and turnings, but can be removed easily without tearing the mouth.

Though still carnivorous, and partial to a trout or two from time to time, it is probably true that we treat trout better than we did, except for those who go in for competitions in killing, which most self-respecting fly fishermen dislike. But our concern does not apply to every creature. Float fishermen are pretty ruthless about maggots and worms.

No scientists, at least none that have come to my notice, have been concerned about the suffering of worms. They must suffer a good deal, one would think, to judge by the wriggle when they are impaled upon a hook and subsequently drowned. In 1870, or thereabouts, an Edinburgh lawyer named Stewart invented a special worm tackle, what one might describe as a crucifix of hooks, which would prolong their lives -and extend their wriggling. No one seems to care much for the welfare of worms. There are a few exceptions, mostly among fly fishermen. John Gay's

> Around the steel no tortured worm shall twine
> No blood of living insect stain my line

is a pleasant reminder that there was a worm protectionist movement which started as long ago as 1720. Admittedly, progress is slow. Not that one should be surprised. The habit of worming, like the worm itself, takes time to die.

IT is, or possibly can be, a sensitive matter to decide whether or not to kill a trout. Those many fisheries in the English Midlands and the South which are artificially stocked, and where the rule is that all trout taken must be killed, forestall anxiety or so one might have thought if it had not been for some of the letters on the subject in the fishing magazines.

The focus of disquiet are fishing competitions on reservoirs between club teams which compete for large sums of money, holidays abroad, silver salvers and cups, and other splendid prizes. These are popular, enjoyable, and have attracted a number of sponsors in recent years, including banks, breweries and cigarette manufacturers.

The question raised by a number of fishermen, essentially an ethical one, is whether it is a good thing or a bad thing to have a competition in killing. A typical letter, referring to some teams fishing at Wimbleball reservoir in Somerset, condemned what the writer called 'the wholesale slaughter of yearling rainbows' and continued:

> I understand that some competitors achieved catches of more than 40 fish, no mean feat, but certainly far from sporting. What on earth would we think if competitions in shooting were to substitute wild pigeons for clays?

The competitors could no doubt have argued, if they had wished, that as the trout were bred specially for the purpose of being killed it was less of an offence to kill 40 farm rainbows than 40 wild salmon or sea trout. Maybe, but it avoids the main question: whether fly fishermen should become competitive, with considerable prizes for those who kill the most. In this we lapse behind the standards of our ancestors. Dame Juliana Berners:

> You must not use this arteful sport for covetousness, merely for the increasing or saving of your money.

Whether there is always scrupulous observance of that advice in the *Treatysse* is doubtful but nevertheless one would have suspected a fairly general reluctance to win a holiday on the Costa Brava over a pile of dead fish, whether they were born free or born to be killed. An American fisherman put it rather well:

> The statement that a man has killed fifty or one hundred trout makes not the slightest impression on the mind, except possibly a slight feeling of disgust.

IT may be unusual to mention it, but fly fishermen who are also bird lovers and bird watchers, do have occasional feelings of guilt. To dress our trout and salmon flies with bird feathers we need not only to scavenge but to kill, or to buy the feathers from others who have done the killing for us. We hunger after such things as mallard and grouse, pheasant and partridge, gamecock and guinea fowl, and many more, and some of the exotic feathers for our salmon flies are no longer available, for they have come from endangered species whose imports are now rightly prohibited. Good, but for us it means privation.

I thought of that the other day during ice-cold weather when two peewits landed in our garden close to our kitchen windows so I could see them quite clearly. With binoculars I felt I could reach out and touch them. Peewits have faces like Chinese mandarins, tall crests, and a green shine on their backs which is like the green of the deep sea. They carried themselves with great arrogance, dibbing here and there into the grass, taking a few dancing steps, a pause, perfectly still, then the head goes down fast, dig dig dig, and up with something quick and swallow. Dig dig, dig, dance dance dance. Fascinating to watch.

Then four more peewits, half a dozen pigeons, and something like fifty or a hundred starlings all arrived with a great fluttering of wings and a good deal of jockeying for pecking order. The worms and the leatherjackets were having a thin time. Even Sammy the dog, coming round the corner from her bone, appeared surprised, possibly incensed, at this invasion of her garden. She made a half-hearted rush at a couple of peewits which took off with a leisurely flap of wings and settled again a little further away. This time the dog left them alone.

We are lucky with our garden, most of it grass and trees and a small pond where mallard come, sheltered from wind, and in a valley by the river surrounded by hills. Water drains from deep inside the hills into the garden and keeps the grass frost-free even in bitter weather, so that in winter especially it is always full of birds, though this winter the peewits were new. I looked at them closely and a little enviously through my glasses. They carried splendid feathers which would make wonderful salmon flies but they were safe with us and seemed to know. Even when I had to go out of the kitchen door towards the garage they did not fly away, but remained, watchful, cautious, yet unafraid.

Down here, in southern England, peewits are called lapwings, and when I looked it up in the bird book I discovered that lapwing comes from the Anglo-Saxon *hleapwince*, meaning run and wink, which goes back to Geatland and no doubt beyond; but in Yorkshire, when I was a boy, we knew no such word, for up there we are Norse, and you can imagine how the colonising Norsemen called the bird what the bird had called to them, *pee -wt*, a sound with a sharp upward *wt*!

I was hopeful some kind bird would shed a feather for me but I have not yet found one and am still waiting for a matching feather to that from a buzzard's tail which was dropped last year, and which would make a wonderful top dressing for a Silver Doctor or a Wilkinson. I must be patient. Feathers will come from somewhere. The only bird I have ever shot was a magpie and that was because it was making war on swallows' nests and I came into the conflict as a swallow's ally. As a result I have enough wing feathers for Butchers for life, though magpie feathers are not to be recommended, being a little too coarse and stiff. That is the extent of my overt predation of birds.

But the dilemma remains. Alternatives are not available. If you want a good wing for a Blue Charm then you must have teal and mallard, and no argument about it, which is why so many of us, I suppose, have gone on to hairwings when we can't get the feathers we want. The process is no doubt irreversible and one day we shall all come to some new synthetic fibre and the skills of an old and antiquated craft will gradually disappear. Very sad. In the meantime when I took dog Sammy for a walk in the garden I searched high and low for one of those sea-green peewit feathers that I thought they might have been generous enough to leave. No good. They had eaten us out of worms and gone away without paying.

FISHERMEN, like Gaul, are divided into three parts. The first group looks upon fishing as a pleasant diversion, to be enjoyed mainly in fine weather and in attractive surroundings. If the fish are co-operative, a trout or two is an added bonus. The second group are passionate and single-minded, to whom the secrets of catching fish are of paramount importance, and whose leisure time is dominated by the desire to become an expert. The third, and much smaller group, are the bug hunters, the angler-entomologists.

The bug hunters are a curious group. Most of them carry little nets, specimen bottles and preservatives, and can be seen rooting about in the shallows of lakes and rivers, turning over stones, shaking bushes, or suddenly capering about as they try to net some unfortunate rarity. It is unwise to engage them in conversation except in the most general terms about the weather or the cricket, for if you mention that you have just seen, say, a medium olive, their eyes will light up and they will at once ask some incomprehensible question about whether you were able to identify it as a *vernus* or a *scambus*, or whatever may be the appropriate Latin names. Avoid this group, if possible, for they can become tedious. On the other hand, these curious men, always probing into fish and insect life, always asking why this should happen, and what is this, and if we do so-and-so what effect will it have, these essentially curious men are those on whom we all depend.

We depended on two men, G. E. M. Skues and Frank Sawyer, for our knowledge of nymph fishing. Our fathers and grandfathers depended on F. M. Halford and Alfred Ronalds for their understanding of natural insects and the way an imitation fly should be fished. In our own time, the way we fish has been strongly influenced by the work of J. R. Harris and John Goddard. All these men belong to the group of angler-entomologists, or perhaps angler-naturalists might be a better description. Only one of them, J. R. Harris, was a professional scientist. The others include a lawyer, a water-keeper, a business man and an ex-parachutist. Unlikely, you would think, that these are the men who guide our rods and tie our flies when we set out for the river or the lake. The fact is that without them we would know nothing of nymphs and how to fish them, very little about the mayflies and the olives, and practically nothing at all about the midge. When we do go out to fish, or sit to tie a fly, they are with us, all the time, guiding, teaching, and increasing our understanding.

From this point of view, it could be that the angler-naturalist is a larger group than we may have at first thought. It is quite possible that dividing fishermen into three categories − the dilettante, the professional, and the bug hunter − though useful enough, may obscure the fact that all of them, to a greater or lesser extent, belong, possibly to their surprise, to the bug hunters and the naturalists. Whenever we look at the water to see what flies are hatching and look in our box to see what might be there, we follow the same road. Our discoveries, it is true, are unlikely to be significant except to ourselves.

FISH, of course, have their own ways of getting even with fishermen. Nothing is more humiliating than to see a fish follow one's artificial downstream, its nose practically touching the hook, only to turn away at the last moment with the most contemptuous expression imaginable. The blow to our pride can be considerable.

It is true there are some who are said to be expert fishermen and are careful to cultivate that reputation, but they must be fairly neurotic and unhappy characters for they know they are always balancing on the razor's edge of defeat. Even if they do take a difficult fish, nymphing between packed weed beds sixty feet off, the next moment they will break on a strike, strike too soon, or put their fly into the bushes. There are no experts who cannot be toppled from their pedestals with the greatest ease by an experienced fish.

That is certainly, if unfortunately, as it should be, for if perfection were possible in fly fishing, if a trout could always be deceived, then boredom might not be too far away. It is the possibility of failure that is so stimulating, and to rely on an unknown but considerable chance so exhilarating as to make all other emotions pale in comparison.

Our conceit, if we have any, and none are entirely immune, must always be moderated by a sense of humility. Then, in compensation, comes the day when we take a two-pounder from an impossible position under a willow and a three-pounder which needed a fly dropped between two weed beds in a space no larger than a tea cup, where conflicting currents provided instant drag, and we begin to imagine we are not so bad as we thought we were. We even begin to pontificate about the right fly, the length of leader, the need to cast the curve, and before we are aware of it consider, or even begin to write, authoritative articles for the magazines. This, if we are not careful, is where the rot sets in and we come to regard ourselves as reasonably skilful. The cure for that illusion, for it is an illusion, is a couple of splendidly blank days.

THERE are monsters in the lake. One never sees them, for they lie deep and do not eat insects, but feed on the stock fish that are newly put in which are unwary and unskilled for they come straight from the hatchery. The old water-keeper, who had ghillied the lake for half a century, told me about the monsters. I took down his words:

> I once saw a trout of three or four pounds taken while I was ghillying a party and we were fishing the evening rise not far off the dam. I netted the fish out and pointed to the marks on it. There were wounds on the back and in the stomach and they were not all that old either. I looked at them for some time and there wasn't much doubt. Something very big had had that trout between its jaws and those were teeth marks. There are no pike in the lake. Imagine the size of a trout that would take another that big in its jaws. That's why I want to get a herring and troll it by the dam. I will one day. I'm sure as I'm here there's a fish down there that'll be on the way to twenty pounds and I'm also sure you'll never get him on the fly.

There is an attraction about monsters which is of course why fish farms are fattening up their rainbows to get them into the monster double-figure class. Somehow these big-bellied brood fish are not the same as a real wild monster. I've only had two monsters in my life: well, a monster and a half, but both terrified me.

The first was a carp hooked by my father in a pond somewhere near North Cave in Yorkshire. We got a glimpse of it close to the surface. It looked yards long. A veritable monster from the deep. My legs went weak at the sight of it. Then the gut parted. The next was a conger eel that weighed 40 pounds plus that I took on a pilchard bait from a boat in the dead of night, just off the Eddystone reef. I got it on board and in the light of a lantern I could see it coming for me across the deck with an open mouth, vicious, determined to attack. Charlie Toms – dear Uncle Charlie – hit it on the tail and turned it with a gaff, but it was a near thing.

I once went fly fishing for shark off the Cornish coast. I don't know what would have happened if a big mako had taken the 'fly' or what would have happened to the trout rod I was using if it had. Did we see a shark? No, but a herring we were trailing on a long line as an attracter for the 'fly' was taken as a reminder that they were there.

I think this is what is so attractive about the thought of monsters. They come out of the unknown. The old sea maps occasionally illustrated sea serpents but the drawings were conventional and the serpents comparatively tame-looking. Your real monster is a very different creature, an image of fear, a provoker of terror.

I MET a man once who told me I ought not to go fishing. He said it was cruel and therefore I was wrong to take pleasure from being cruel. He was a nice man, led by various complexities into being a lay preacher and a vegetarian, a combination which together must be regarded as fairly formidable if one comes across them in argument.

I pointed out that Jesus's disciples were fishermen before they became fishers of men. This was no problem to a lay preacher, indeed he leapt upon the point with joy, because he said they did not fish for pleasure or sport or relaxation, or any reason of that kind, but to give people food, for they were an important part of the organisation which provided the loaves and the fishes. In the case of our modern rod and line fishermen they did it for pleasure and not as part of the nation's food supply.

We then went into the question of what professional fisherman actually did when they caught fish, and how the fish were brought in on the trawl, lifted inboard, the purse opened, and several hundredweight of fish dropped into the hold, stunned, suffocated, bruised, drowning in air, left slowly to die or in some cases gutted alive.

One might say, up to a point, that the trawlerman got some pleasure from the catch, for it would pay the mortgage and clothe the bairns, and certainly that would be a point of pleasure or of satisfaction, however pleasure was defined, but might it also not contain a certain modicum of cruelty to the fish. To my surprise my lay preacher friend agreed. I can quote his words for I can still hear him saying them: 'As soon as I knew how cod were caught,' he said, 'I gave up eating fish fingers.'

There was nothing further to say, nothing to explore, no possible excuse for continuing. For a man willingly to give up eating the food he liked and face the rest of his life on a diet based mainly on the soya bean is the stuff of sainthood.

A fact perhaps worth mentioning, for it is something my lay preacher was not able to appreciate, is that a good many fly fishermen, quite possibly a large majority of experienced fly fishermen, gain no pleasure from killing and find it distasteful and indeed repugnant. We come up here, of course, against the carnivore and the turning of the blind eye. We do not as a rule see the activity that goes on inside abattoirs or on the boat decks of trawlers so that when we enjoy our roast beef or smoked salmon we do so in a way that seals us off from the past, from any thought of killing or bloodshed or pain that have brought such pleasures to us. The fisherman, landing-net in hand, faces the reality in one way, the vegetarian in another.

91

Bright waters

WE had to fish our March Browns downstream. We had
tried fishing them upstream but the wind was so strong
they were blown back. The temperature was low, our hands
were becoming numb; then came the rain and hit the river like
bullets. No good going on. The Usk had defeated us. We crept
back over the sodden field to the Abergavenny road, got
thankfully into the car, turned the engine and the heater on full
blast and began to thaw. We drank whisky, nibbled something,
and discussed what we were going to do. We then saw a salmon
fisherman crossing the field, coming towards us, returning to his
car. He had also given up. We were not surprised.

His car was just behind ours in the parking place by the side
of the road and as he passed us we lowered our window and
asked him how he had done. 'No salmon,' he said, 'but if you're
after trout there's a hatch of fly and they're rising all over the
place.'

It sounded impossible. It was still raining, though not so
heavily as before, and the wond had dropped a little. We

thanked him and looked at each other, at the rain spattering against the windscreen, and felt considerable reluctance.

'Is it worth it?'
'What do you think?'
'Perhaps for . . .'
'Ten minutes?'

The salmon fisherman had told the truth. There was a hatch, of something that looked uncommonly like a March Brown. Some of the flies were struggling in the water, unable to fly because of the rain, but others were coming up all the time, and the trout, the big wild brown trout of Usk, were after them.

All that one remembered afterwards was the way the rises were exploding all over the river, here, there, across the far side, under our bank, in the main flow of the stream, in the whorls of the eddies, and trout were taking the flies with a savage abandon; then the exhilaration of putting our own flies on the water in front of the rising fish, watching for the take, missing it, casting again, and again, seeing the trout we were casting for taking a natural and ignoring our own, then unexpectedly taking ours, feeling the sudden intensity of battle. It was as if both of us, man and fish, were taking part in an old ritual.

Scientists, or at least one or two of them, have explained that at such moments our deep subconscious past takes over from our conscious present and that instinctively, for it is indeed our deepest instinct, we return to what we were in a time before recorded history, or as Howard Marshall once so admirably put it, we shake hands with the caveman. Certainly it feels not unlikely that some great traumatic experience overtakes us, for it is noticeable, and certainly was that day on the Usk.

93

ON the Wharfe, the olives hatch fast. I saw one close to my waders. Up came the nymph, I could see it rise to the surface, for I happened to be looking down at that moment. It seemed as if it broke the water for nothing more than a split second and then the fly was out of the nymphal case and away in the air. Bingo! Up and away without waiting.

The week before, or maybe a fortnight, I had been on the Itchen and had seen the hatch of a medium olive. I saw it appear on the water where there had been no fly the instant before. At the moment of hatching the wings seemed to be ready for take-off but there was no sign of the fly doing so. It rode the stream, gracefully, flicking its wings occasionally, once, possibly twice, making a trial flight but nothing much more than a hop before landing back on the water.

The fly drifted down towards me and I watched it go past and drift down almost out of sight round the bend when there was a sudden *plop* and that was the end of it. Why do flies on the chalk streams behave like this when clearly they have the ability to fly long before they wish to do so? That particular olive on the Itchen must have drifted ten yards at least downstream before the trout had him. Maybe twelve or fourteen yards. Whatever the distance, it was a long way. Why did it take its time? Did it like going for a sail on the nice smooth water? Is it something to do with the nature of the water, the rough water of the Wharfe stimulating an instant take-off? There are theories but I have no valid explanation.

To return to the Itchen and the long drift of the fly. It was at this time, so far as I remember, that I rose four fish in succession and hooked none of them. One rise was clearly a last-minute refusal, for I saw the fish turn away. As he turned he broke the surface, which, if I had not seen the fish, would have made me tighten in the belief that the fly had been taken. But no, it was certainly a refusal and perhaps if I had been able to see the other three rises one or more might have been the same. The reason, one suspects, is that in all these cases, when a fly spends a long time on the water, the trout have an equally long time, or very nearly an equally long time, to have a look and see what kind

94

of a fly it is and whether this is the particular kind they like. The water is shallow, on the whole, and provided detritus is not clouding it, has an exceptional clarity. It is, as they say, as clear as crystal and flows as slowly and as stately as a queen's barge.

Drop an artificial fly on water of that quality and even the lightest of nylon will crack on the surface like splintering a glass window. It is not surprising that on the Itchen the trout are reasonably sophisticated and take their time examining whatever may be offered. It is also not surprising that quite a few fishermen, myself most emphatically included, find themselves at a loss from time to time, quite uncertain whether the trout are taking the emerging nymph, a Black Gnat, or whatever it is that is not the medium olives that are visibly on the water. In the case of my four trout which had either refused my fly or come short and missed it, there was no doubt something queer was going on.

I should have known. Here and there among the olives there were iron blues and that seemed to be the answer. At least it was an explanation, and an excuse to change the fly. I like winged iron blues but there were only hackled patterns in my box, so one makes the best of what one has, rebuking oneself at the same time for coming so unprepared. I remember that as I took off the olive and knotted on the iron blue I found myself tingling with anticipation. After fishing for many years one ought to have got used to it, but one never does.

The first cast was blown off course. There was a nasty crosswind and the trout I had my eye on was in position just beyond and a little to the side of a drooping willow that shaded the centre of the stream. To get near, one had to creep a little further than one should, taking cover behind a screen of nettles, casting low and sideways. The next cast went into the nettles behind me so I had to crawl back again to release the fly, get stung, and crawl up again to the right position. This time I had loops of line round my boots and draped on some rather strong brambles.

I suppose the trout must have seen the disturbance, the shaking of my screen of nettles, the rising humps of back and

95

body as I struggled to free the line, the waving of rod and arms. Eventually, when I settled down with all under control, the trout had stopped rising. So I waited where I was. I got cramp. The knee I was using to kneel on began to hurt. I changed to the other knee. My hands were hurting from the nettles. Feeling I must do something, I cast to where the trout had been rising and put my fly into the willow.

About half an hour later when I had put on a new fly and a new length of nylon and crawled back through the nettles again to my former place, which now looked as if it had been trampled by cows, the trout was in position and rising steadily. I was pretty exhausted by this time and not at my best, so my first cast was horribly wide of the mark, fortunately splashing down near to my own bank and not the willow. The next cast was miraculously good. The little fly floated down for a yard, maybe a yard and a half, and a wave came over it and down it went under a ridge of water, the rings spreading out. The fish, a wild brown, was not big, but had a perfection of colour that marks the true Itchen fish. I held him in the water, getting stung from more nettles, released him, and he was away at once with a flick of his tail.

I had worked hard for that fish.

FISHING the evening rise is one of the more infuriating aspects of fly fishing. Trout will suddenly rise all over the river about the time when the sun is reddening and enlarging and beginning to dip behind the trees. No one will have the faintest idea what the trout are taking for no fly is visible on the water or in the air.

The standard tactic for the evening rise is to start with a spinner and if that does not seem to work follow with a Blue-winged Olive and ultimately a Sedge; or contrariwise one starts with a BWO, goes on to the spinner and then the Sedge. In either case, it doesn't seem to make much difference. All offerings are ignored.

Now comes a subtle approach, a size 20 Black Gnat, or something of that kind, tied on nylon so fine that if it is taken at all, which is doubtful, the nylon will be snapped like a thread. Having tried everything, one goes back to the BWO or the spinner that one used in the first place. It is now taken confidently by a good fish. In our surprise we strike too fast and pull the fly out of its mouth.

At this stage, with the light now rapidly going, we see what we are convinced is a Sedge and tie on a good Red Palmer with over-hasty fingers. A long cast to the far bank and a quick *pull-pull* and the fly is chased by a huge fish which takes it and vanishes into the weed. Almost at once the line comes back to us with that ominous curl of nylon at the end which suggests that the knot has pulled out.

In one way, we must consider ourselves lucky to have risen fish at all, though that is not much consolation as we wander home fishless. There is no doubt about our feeling of incompetence. We had no idea what the fish were taking. If they changed to the spinner from the BWO, we had no idea of it. The one that took the spinner might have done it by mistake and although a fish did chase the Palmer, it was our fault that he came off. A miserable exhibition all round.

The truth is, if we are honest with ourselves, that for most of the time we haven't had the faintest idea what we ought to have been doing. It is at this point that we are saved from complete despair by the sudden realisation that what we did wrong was to use a Sherry Spinner instead of the Lunn's.

IF there is ever a chance of fishing the fly within a bus ride from Piccadilly it will probably be on the Cray, a chalk stream that rises at Orpington, flows through St Mary Cray, under the main road to North Cray, Bexley, and Crayford, then into the River Darent and so finally to the Thames.

Most London rivers have been badly polluted and some are still open sewers, or rather closed, for many have been put underground, partly for the convenience of builders, partly for the benefit of the general public.

With the Cray there are signs of a revival. David Martin, a London architect, who spent five years exploring the city's lost rivers, has high hopes of the Cray. He found the upper reaches clear, with clean gravel, and a good growth of ranunculus and starwort which provide suitable breeding places for fly. A stocking of brown trout fly has been successful. Small boys with worms and crystal hooks are no doubt on their way to the Cray if not already there.

London commuters who travel from Waterloo westward are probably familiar with Wandsworth, and may even have glimpsed, briefly, a frothy-looking sewer between concrete walls as the train passes over a small viaduct. This is also a chalk stream, the Wandle, which at one time was a favourite river of Izaak Walton and also, surprisingly, of Nelson, who had a large estate at Merton and was a dedicated fly fisherman, so dedicated that when he lost his right arm at Santa Cruz he set out to teach himself to cast with his left.

The river produced many fine trout of three pounds or more and in 1868, when F. M. Halford fished the Wandle, it was still of fine quality. Indeed, it was on the Wandle that Halford, then aged 24, had his first experience of fishing the dry fly.

But all that is past, the river is now highly urbanised, and even though some trout have been put into it and have apparently survived it is doubtful whether fly fishing will ever again take place. At least in the upper reaches it flows through pleasant gardens, so it gives pleasure to many, which is more than can be said of some of London's other rivers. The Holburn and the Fleet are part of the city's sewerage system, remembered only by names they have given to the streets above their courses, Holborn and Fleet Street, but the Westbourne brook has had something of a happy ending. It feeds the Serpentine in Hyde Park.

Rivers, says David Martin, must never again be treated as sewers and diverted underground. Properly preserved and flowing in a natural state, they are a joy to everyone and a perfect antidote to the pressures of city life.

FLY FISHERMEN are generally well camouflaged. Indeed, some are so well camouflaged that a senior member of the Flyfishers' who fished the Kennet at Chamberhouse had the reputation of being practically indistinguishable from a tree. Those who conceal themselves as well as this are among the more experienced of their kind. It is sad that so many fishermen, especially on the clear rivers of the chalk, and especially beginners, seem to have little or no idea that the mere sight of them can put a fish down.

The worst example I remember was of a fisherman on the Test at Timsbury who was wearing a vivid red shirt under a light-coloured fishing waistcoat. It was a new waistcoat and his tackle was new as well. The shirt was visible a quarter of a mile away and, as we approached, the colour became so strong it seemed to possess that kind of fluorescence that advertisers use on posters to compel attention. We were compelled.

It was sad. He was flailing away, standing up on a high bank without any cover, the line going down crooked on the water with a heavy splash. If there had been a fish there once, there was no fish there now. Any self-respecting trout would have fled in terror. We came up behind him and made the usual wide detour to go round, but even before we had begun to do so he had sensed our presence and was on the alert. He half turned.

'Do keep away. You'll put them down.'

'Yes, of course.'

99

We made an even wider detour, getting well into the brambles. There was nothing we could do or say and it was best to give him a wide berth. He had an authoritative and arrogant-sounding voice and was clearly the kind of man who knew how to do things and was used to being obeyed.

We saw him once more, in the car park at lunch time. He was complaining about the fishing to one of our fellow rods. 'No bloody fish in the river,' he said, and got into a large and powerful open sports car and drove off in an angry spattering of gravel. We saw why he was wearing a red shirt. It matched the colour of his car.

'FISHING for amiable and relatively easy fish,' said my nice American. He had come from fishing one of the prime beats of the Test. He had enjoyed himself but the fish he had caught were from the hatcheries.

I wish I could have taken him to the Border streams. There are not so many wild fish there now as there used to be. Over-fishing and farm pollution is killing them off fast. But there are enough. And nobody stocks those rivers, at least no one did when I was last there some years back. I always remember my first meeting with trout in the Jed.

Distance may have lent enchantment to the memory, but I think not. I was driving up from London to Edinburgh on the old east coast route on my way, as a reporter, to a rather dull political conference and I didn't like the prospect all that much. Conferences can be dull. I crossed the Border on the old A68 and, some miles short of Jedburgh, saw a little river on my right.

There was something rather beautiful and unusual about this river. It ran under a large red sandstone cliff on the far side and on the near bank was an attractive-looking meadow with short, sheep-cropped grass. An idyllic kind of a place, I thought, and stopped off in Jedburgh to make enquiries. A newsagent and tobacconist directed me to a bank manager further up the street, a friendly bank manager, who gave me a day ticket and good advice, for he was secretary of the local angling club and knew the water well. The Jed Water, he called it. It is one of the feeder streams of the Teviot which in turn feeds the Tweed. So I went to the Jed Water. There was a rod in the boot of my car. I had half a day. Never in all my life have I been so humiliated and frustrated by trout as I was on the Jed. It was quite extraordinary. I walked across the meadow and in front of me was this exquisitely shaped sandstone cliff and on my own bank a fringe of grass which hid the little stream on the far side. Gradually, as I walked on, the stream came into view. It was very low and very clear, so clear you could see the pebbles from one bank to the other. I could also see the fish, maybe half a dozen or a dozen in that particular pool, and as soon as my head came over that fringe of grass the fish vanished. I had never seen trout move so fast. *Flick, flick, jigger, jigger, jigger,* and they were gone.

I tried everything. I crept, I crawled, I hid myself under bushes, I lay flat on my stomach and cast sideways with my rod parallel to the water. Not a fish came. I tried them with dry fly, I tried them with wet fly, I tried them with nymph. Nothing at all. Not one fish. Not one rise. Nothing.

Dear Jed Water. One day I shall come back.

A touch of magic

THE trout season sidles in rather than opens. There is no fixed day throughout the country, as there is with grouse, which you know, without troubling, is the day when you can take out your rod and cast a fly. Nothing so simple. There are or were at least six official opening days for the trout season in England during March, three in April, and one or possibly two in May, and there could be more.

An untidy system, you might say, and so it is, for there seems no good reason at all why the Dove should be a couple of days later than the Dart, or for that matter why worming should be allowed on one and not on the other. But then the whole complex pattern has grown up from parish to parish, river by river, before it became area by area or even region by region, chopping and changing over the past hundred years or so in a way that is a muddle and a mystery to all foreigners, and even, though not always, to some of the English.

Genetic engineering has now turned everything upside down as fish farmers produce sexless rainbows, or lady rainbows that are disinterested in sex: I am a little uncertain whether it is one or the other. However, as the result of tampering with their genes the trout are now, so we are told, in condition all the year round, more or less, so that a close season is no longer needed. On the other hand, it might be that a close season is needed by the fisherman. Fishing the drift in winter across Rutland Water or Grafham in a high wind and sub-zero temperatures might not be to everybody's taste. One never knows. The Scots are reputed to break the ice for their first salmon of the year in February but then the Scots are a hardy race.

I find the big reservoirs formidable enough at any time of the year and though I have read many of the best books on how to fish them, I am still rather at a loss when faced with these great waters. A bank fisherman, especially, seems dwarfed by them, which is perhaps why fishermen huddle together so often, almost shoulder to shoulder, all casting away and double-hauling for dear life. They cannot be blamed for wanting to cast as far as possible when a couple of miles of water are between them and the opposite bank. These inland seas are apt to dwarf our human endeavours, belittling them, putting us tiny creatures very much in our place.

Fishing the drift makes us feel a little better. After all, we are going somewhere, even if the water a mile away is just as empty of fish as the water a mile behind. Never mind that, we are travelling, we are covering fresh water all the time, and there is always the chance of a monster lurking in the waves ahead. It is the possibility of the unexpected that keeps us going. With a fish in the morning, perhaps, and one in the afternoon, we may feel we have not done too badly after all.

But when the evening comes, the last hour or so of the day,

when midges hatch and sticklebacks come into the shallows to spawn, bank fishing erupts into sudden glory. It is difficult to think of any fishing more exciting than these late-evening rises. In the village on the hill the lights in the cottages sparkle like stars, coming out one by one, to make companionable the darkling world. The clouds above the hill are slowly lit with purple and orange from the setting sun. The whole of the lake begins to reflect the purple and the orange and the starlight, and in the midst of this blaze of colour the trout start to rise. It happens rarely, but when it does fishermen are among the privileged few who see the changing beauty of the lake and the hunger of the trout and know that for a brief hour they are near paradise.

FISHING textbooks, being written by intensely practical men, sometimes omit to remind us if their authors think of it at all, that fly fishing needs to have a touch of magic about it if we are to enjoy it to the full. Most of that magic, though by no means all, is provided by our surroundings.

For me, Blagdon is one such magical place. I fished there when I was very young, and when I go back there now it recreates much of the careless happiness of youth. I fished there with my father, and briefly with my grandfather, so they are close to me again, bringing a sad nostalgia, yet an inward pleasure. Here are the same trees I saw as a boy, the same dark and mysterious waters, the same green hills. It is like coming home.

Here I listened to tales of monster fish and great fishermen, giants of time past with names like a ring of bells. Here I learned of the mysterious Blagdon boil, when the big fish come in from the depths to hunt the sticklebacks in the shallows, monstrous trout of a size no one had ever imagined, trout that would take out all a man's line and all the backing and snap it like fine cotton thread.

The great days of Blagdon, which my grandfather knew, were shortly after it was opened for fishing in 1904. The lake was first filled three years before. In those days it was fished mainly, perhaps entirely, by the directors of Bristol Waterworks and their friends. The water was fertile and the trout grew to enormous size. This, from *The Field* of May 6, 1905:

> The sport experienced last year is continuing this season on an even more awe-inspiring scale. On Tuesday last those well-known anglers, Mr R. L. White and Mr R. C. Hardy Corfe, fished the reservoir with the fly (the March Brown) and accounted for 20 fish with an aggregate weight of 91½ lb. The weights are thus recorded: 2 lb 12 oz, 3 lb, 3 lb, 3 lb, 3 lb 4 oz, 3 lb 12 oz, 4 lb, 4 lb 6 oz, 4 lb 8 oz, 4 lb 8 oz, 4 lb 10 oz, 4 lb 10 oz, 4 lb 11 oz, 4 lb 12 oz, 4 lb 12 oz, 5 lb, 5 lb 8 oz, 5 lb 12 oz, 7 lb 4 oz and 8 lb 4 oz. The last fish is stated to be the heaviest so far taken from the reservoir with a fly.

A fisherman of that time, Ernest Phillips, said it was not uncommon to hook two fish at the same time, weighing perhaps 3 lb or 4 lb each, one on the dropper, one on the point. Few fishermen were about, perhaps one or two in a day, and they left their rods ready made up in the anglers' hut when they went home or back to the Saloon bar of the Live And Let Live after the evening rise. The rod-rests are still there, in the ceiling of the anglers' hut, but nobody leaves their rods there now. In those days it was more of a club.

The two bailiffs, Donald Carr and Laurie Williamson, and Willie Cox and my father, Herbert, known to everyone as Bert or Bertie, used to go out in a boat to fish the evening rise. Sometimes Laurie was at the oars by himself, but if Donald Carr came as well, one of the two ghillies fished. They used sea-trout flies on what was known as a limber rod, mostly a soft greenheart of 11 ft or 12 ft, with a cast of two or three flies, Greenwell, Pennell, March Brown, Mallard and Claret, or a Blue and Silver. They drifted, casting ahead on a short line, bobbing the flies through the waves. When the takes came, they did so with a great smash. Willie Cox would say: 'We never got much less than a three-pounder, often four or five-pounders.'

They fished the fly mostly during the evening rise, almost always from a boat in loch style. If they fished from the bank, especially during the day, they used a spinner, a drop minnow, a sprat, a wooden Devon, or something of that kind. My grandfather disliked the new methods of fishing pupae and nymph imitations from the bank, a method pioneered by another Blagdon regular, Dr Bell, of Wrington. Bell would spoon out his trout and tie patterns to imitate the insects he found. He was the first to tie famous patterns such as the Blagdon Buzzer, the Grenadier, and the Amber Nymph.

Willie Cox didn't approve. 'Not fly fishing,' he would say, puffing out his long, drooping moustache with an indignant explosion of air. 'Not fly fishing at all. Fishing bloody worms and things. Might as well fish maggot! Pah!' *Puff, puff.* 'Not sporting.'

I was sometimes hard put to discover my grandfather's definition of 'sporting'. I came to suspect that it was one of those movable words that he applied to anything new and different. When spinning was banned in one part of the lake, he was very angry. That was unsporting. He immediately set to and designed a minnow-fly, made out of wool and tinsel, which was as long as a Devon, even longer, which he cast prodigious distances with a salmon rod.

106

When someone told him that was unsporting because it was just the same as using a spinner, he was very angry indeed. 'Bugger you!' he said, dancing up and down on the bank, puffing his moustache, 'Bugger Bristol Waterworks! Bugger the lot of you!'

There was no arguing with Grandpa Cox when he was like that. In the old days he might have made a good pirate. His natural bravura style found little scope in the rigid social patterns of his time. My father thought him irresponsible, which was probably true, for Grandpa Cox was either out fishing for most of the week – he would sell his catch to a Clifton fishmonger – or, if he was not fishing, he would be painting scenery for the shows at the Theatre Royal. In those days the theatre was called the Old Gaff and had music-hall turns most weeks, with an occasional melodrama such as *East Lynne*. Grandpa must have been a reasonable artist, for he held his job there for a long time – as long as I can remember. Most theatre folk in those days were said to have loose morals, and Grandpa Cox had a great reputation as a womaniser. It was said that when he was at home he used to chase the maids round the house. In my schoolboy imagination I used to visualise a great deal of scampering up and down stairs and screams and giggles of delight. I suppose I envied him.

But the magic of Blagdon has never been better captured than by a huge, burly 6-ft 4-in bass-baritone, a concert artist with an international reputation: Harry Plunket Greene, who fished the lake for many years in the 1910s and '20s. This is what he wrote:

There is not a lovelier sight (*pace* Ramsbury and Hurstbourne Priors in buttercup time) in England than Blagdon from the Butcombe end at sundown, with the tiny town straggling up the steep hillside like a Bavarian village, the red roofs of the houses peeping out of the thick orchards (with never a Methodist Chapel to shock the artist's eye), and the evening sunlight setting the windows of the old church aglow and flushing with purple-pink the glassy surface of the lake. There is a stillness here that belongs to no other valley. You can hear

107

the 'plop' of the big trout far out, half-a-mile away. You can talk to your friend across the water when the sun is down without ever raising your voice, and hear the scream of his reel in the blackness, and Blagdon is about seven miles round and he may be half the length of the lake from you.

But the dominant impression in my mind is the lovely colour of the evening light upon the valley as you face it looking east. It has a crimson velvet glow that hangs like an aura on the meadows and makes the shores and the scolloped hills burn with fires. It is Devonshire clay here, and the whole landscape warms pink and deepens to purple-black as the sun sinks low.

And I know, too, that there was once a witch in the valley, and that they drowned her when they let the water in; and one night as I grope my way home in the dark I shall stumble on Hansel and Gretel asleep on the grass in a mist of white angels, with the myriad million stars of the Milky Way and the golden lights of Blagdon shining on their heads and winking in the watery glass at their feet.

Volcano tea

NOT for years had I seen a Volcano Kettle, not since I was a boy scout rubbing two sticks together and, with the lack of success, having to make do with paraffin and matches. The Volcano Kettle was introduced to us by our scoutmaster, whose name I cannot now recall, but whom I remember for the kettle and for the peculiar shape of his bare knees. Adult knees have a fascination for small boys. They are so different from their own, or they were, because nowadays small boys seem to wear trousers and not shorts. But all this was a long time ago, and it was fifty years or more before the Volcano Kettle reappeared in my life on the shores of an Irish lough.

We had landed, or the ghillie had landed us, on a vagrant shore of gorse bushes and wild fuchsia, of low harsh grass, peat bog, and limestone boulders. It was an empty, wild and tangled place, yet somehow comfortable and reassuring, though it was unlikely to have seen a human, apart from fishermen and ghillies, for half a thousand years. As we opened the picnic basket and took out the plates of cold chicken, and salad, and foil-wrapped home-made cake, he produced, as if by magic, the Volcano Kettle.

He filled the outside container of the kettle with water from the lough and the inside compartment with chippity bits of dead gorse branches. These he doused with petrol and then he threw a lighted match on to them from afar. The petrol puffed into flame, the dry chips of branches inside the kettle caught fire, and smoke poured out from the little chimney. The water in the outer compartment took warmth from the fire inside, and within five minutes or so was boiling. There is nothing quite like Volcano tea.

ONE of the great features of fishing the lough was to be out with James O'Hara. He handled the boat like a master – as indeed he was – and he knew the lough as well as he knew the way of his fields. He made no useless chatter, no idle gossip, told no unlikely tales. He kept himself well to himself; but when he did say anything, it was slow and thoughtful and to the point. A good ghillie can make your fishing, just as a bad or a difficult one can ruin the day without trying. James was good and the fishing was good, even though the skies poured out that soft, warm and penetrating Mayo rain for most of the week, except when it was blowing a gale. But even with the gale he had a trick with the oars that kept the boat on a level drift at the right speed, and no drogue to help, either. He disliked drogues. He didn't need them.

The sea-trout, fresh from the sea, came savagely to our flies. Some we gave to James and some we kept for ourselves, which is the right and proper way to behave, though we kept the largest, just under 4 lb, which fought like a salmon three times the weight. It would be unwise to fish those loughs with a line less than 7 lb or 8 lb breaking-strain. We used 9-ft carbon graphite rods, not too stiff, a point-fly and two droppers, casting a short line ahead of the drift in the traditional way.

Traditional, too, were the flies. They were not at all the neat-winged, brightly coloured Peter Rosses and Dunkelds which you might see fished on Maree or Hope, but shaggy dark-coloured Irish patterns that Kingsmill Moore writes about so well. Some five or six gained James's approval, and though I daresay others might have done as well, we stuck to these, changing them from time to time, point to bob, middle to point, as the fancy pleased.

Two splendid patterns, both dark and suitably shaggy, the Bibio and the Bluebottle, were both admirable on the bob, making a fine wake as they came scuttering and flickering over the waves back to the boat. We learned a little trick of this from James. You make quite a short cast, not more than twice or three times the length of the rod, but as soon as the flies hit the water, you lift the rod high. This brings the flies to the surface and as soon as this happens, with the rod high, you begin the retrieve. This skitters the bob-fly over and through the tops of the waves all the way back from where they have entered the water until within a yard or so of the boat. A fish will often follow the flies, attracted by the wake made by the bob, and may well take close to the boat, sometimes the bob but often one of the others. What you need − and this is what brings up so many fish − is a bob-fly that bobbles from start to finish, all the time the flies are on the water.

In August, one of the great bob-flies is the Daddy, quite a big fly, with half-a-dozen knotted legs made from the fibres of a cock pheasant's tail. It looks the living image of the natural daddy-long-legs, and is fished to scutter on the top of the water on the windward side of the lough where the crane-flies are blown.

Some of the Irish — James is not one of them — use two of the natural flies impaled through the body on a hook. I find this an unpleasant thing to do, and cruel, and will have none of it.

In reserve, as it were, though all of them took fish, were the Kingsmill, the Claret Bumble, and the Green Peter. The first two were the inventions of T. C. Kingsmill Moore, and the last pattern goes back well into history. For the fly-dresser it could be pre-history, for all we know of its origins. The Green Peter suggests a sedge, rather like our own Woodcock and Green, though without the tag.

Let me, while I think of it, record the origin of another famous Irish fly, the Bibio. The story goes that Major Charles Roberts, a retired army officer who lived not far from the Burrishoole fishery in Mayo, was one day teaching his daughters how to tie flies. He was tying a fly himself, winding black wool on the shank. In the middle of the shank he tied in several turns of orange wool, and then more black wool up to the head. He then tied on a black hackle and palmered it down to the tail.

He looked at the fly and thought it was good. The orange band gleamed out through the black hackles in a most takeable way. He tried it and his friends tried it, and they also found it was good. So they asked him what it was called. He thought for a bit and said he didn't know, but he thought he might call it the Bibio. They asked why Bibio? He didn't know that either, but he'd seen the name somewhere and thought it was rather a nice name for a fly.

Indeed, it is a nice name for a fly, for it is the family name, the genus, of a large group of flies which include the hawthorn, *Bibio marci*, and the black gnat, *Bibio johannes*. He chose well.

ONE of the greatest fishermen I ever met was an Irishman. I never saw him fish, but I read his book and met him three times and talked into the small hours. Kingsmill Moore, who tied the Kingsmill and the Bumbles, is still remembered by the

Irish. They use his flies and treasure his book, the one he wrote on fishing, which captures more than any other the spirit and feeling of the people and places of Ireland. It is sad that Kingsmill Moore and Jamesie and the Big House are no more, but that is the way of things, and there are still the lakes and the hills of Mayo and Connemara to visit and to be a part of, if only for a while.

K.M. – he was always called K.M. – had a great deal to say about flies. He had a judicial way of looking at them, a fine, analytical look with clear, grey eyes under heavy eyebrows, the kind of eyebrows that used to be called beetling, for one reason or another. If I had been in the dock while he was on the bench – he was a great judge – I doubt if I would have been comfortable under that appraising look.

I have never known a man, not even Skues, who could set out the qualities and uses of the wet fly as clearly as did K.M. It is difficult to remember all the details, but you are the better for having read them. They become a part of you, and the clear judgment of his mind seeps into your own, so that even if you do not remember what he has said, your judgment is somehow improved by his example.

K.M.'s knowledge of so many things was considerable and profound, and on flies and fishing none was better. I mentioned the Bluebottle as taking fish on the lough. There was not a fly that he didn't know:

Blue Body Black Hackle is an Irish name for a fly which has been used by generations of fishermen. In my youth no fisherman in Wicklow was without it. In Scotland it is known as Cairn's Fancy, in the north of England it is identical with one of the dressings of Broughton's Point, and without any name attached it was one of Stewart's winged flies. Starling wing, black hackle, and a body of dark gentian blue – sometimes a purple claret – ribbed with flat silver, it will kill from the first day to the last on any mountain stream. Dressed larger, and called the Bluebottle, it kills well on mountain lakes.

113

And that is a fact, though the Bluebottle we had in Mayo was without the wing and was hackled from eye to bend. I am defeated by K.M., because once I start quoting the man, I go on quoting him. I cannot resist it. Here is his description of a Corrib boatman, a perfect gem of a piece of prose:

> Jamesie was a red Celt. Time had sown sand over his flaming hair and taken some of the colour from the blue of his eyes, but his back was still as flat and straight as a door, and he walked delicately, like a cat. He admitted to being eighty, and Jimmy put him down as being more, but he was a man whose age could not be reckoned by the years. He was the leader of the two, which seemed odd, for Jimmy owned the boat. But Jamesie owned the lake, if not indeed the earth. He had struck his bargain with life and it contented him. Old he might be, but he was savouring his old age with as much enjoyment as he had his youth, still vital, interested and more than a little mischievous. As a Corrib boatman he had begun and as a Corrib boatman he hoped to end. There had however been a period of wandering when his horizon had not been bound by the hills of Galway and Mayo, when he had sailed the seven seas and gasconaded it in the great ports of the world. Tired of his travels, Ulysses had returned to Ithica with tales of strange monsters and the blue Sympleglades. He was a little feared for his sharp wits and tongue, a great deal respected for his skill and knowledge. Any one of the boatmen could dap and troll, but only Jamesie was expert with the wet fly, and he enjoyed in addition that singular prestige which fishermen who cannot tie their own flies are accustomed to accord to those who can.

We shall have to wait a long time indeed to find a man born who can write as well as that, for it has in it all the quality of Synge and the rest of the Irish. If you have ever had the pleasure of seeing Cyril Cusack in *The Playboy of the Western World*, you will know exactly what I mean.

HOW does one educate a trout? Scientists and fishermen seem, for the moment anyway, to disagree on the subject but this may be more apparent than real. It depends what one means by educate. That is the crux of the matter or, if you like, the stumbling block.

There is good evidence, especially from catch-and-release waters, that after being caught several times a trout becomes wary of artificial flies. From some of the Catskill rivers in America come reports that the big trout there, which may have been caught and released as many as a dozen or more times over the years, have become quite impossible to take on flies unless they are so small that the hook is almost invisible in the dressing. They also know about nylon, because, apparently, any sign of a line on the water brings a refusal. A nylon point will have to be exceptionally fine and very long indeed. One of the fishermen of the Beaverkill, Art Lee, uses a point longer than his rod.

One can understand a Catskill trout's feelings: here we go again, taking a nice big juicy fly from the surface and it turns round and bites and drags you all around the pool until you are completely tired out and are rescued only at the very last moment by some pink things that take the fly out of your jaw and let you go free. Next time, boyo, take one of those smaller flies. They don't bite.

It may all be rather anthropomorphic, but the reasoning, or the conditioning, or whatever you like to call it, could be along those lines. The worry is whether the offspring of the present-day Catskill trout are going to inherit this conditioning from their parents. In such a case, and if that could happen, we would be breeding a strain of trout with an inbuilt hereditary antipathy to eating flies. The thought of permanent bottom-feeding trout would be the end of fly fishing as we know it. However, the latest from the science boys is not at all discouraging. They say that for trout to acquire an inherited anti-fly instinct might take a period of indoctrination longer than we first thought, give or take something like a couple of hundred thousand years. On the

115

other hand they might not acquire it at all.

We should be all right for the time being.

THE river was rather like parts of the Dart, high wooded banks, a rough, fast-flowing stream, waterfalls, rocks bunched at the heads of pools, and water so clear you could see the flash of trout in the shallows. You could well imagine you were on the Dart except for the printed notice to fishermen posted on a tree by the bridge. It read:

> This is a fish for fun stream. All fish caught must be handled carefully and returned immediately to the stream. Only artificial flies or lures with one single barbless hook permitted. Possession of fish at any time is illegal.

Fish for fun gives the clue to where you are: one of the trout streams in the United States organised by the state game and fishery department as a no-kill area, to preserve the stocks of wild fish. There are many such rivers. This one was the Rapidan in Virginia. By the banks of another river, the Beaverkill in the Catskills, we talked to a professional guide. I took a note of what he said:

> This part is a no-kill stream. You have to fish it with a point maybe ten or fifteen feet long, very fine, with small flies. After these trout have been caught fourteen or fifteen times they become very difficult. They learn. From my point of view they become a better fish if they're caught more than once.
>
> In another part there's a three trout limit. You can take them under ten inches but not over. Each river, indeed each part of a river, is managed on an independent basis. We're going very heavily into wild trout management. We've got

here the potential for the greatest fly fishing in the world. One thing we don't want to do, will never do, is stock. We don't want hatchery dummies.

The fishermen we talked to were all contemptuous of these 'hatchery dummies', and in a curious way felt sad that most of the English chalk streams were now stocked. To them there was nothing like a wild trout. Streams which had to be stocked they thought of as badly exploited or badly managed. Nevertheless they were fascinated by our stories of English rivers. They thought our system of private ownership of fishing was elitist and they had a curious picture of the English dry fly fisherman wearing knickerbockers, Norfolk jacket, a Sherlock Holmes hat, and smoking a pipe.

With us, you see, we don't have this classic type of English dry fly fisherman. Over here a real dry fly purist can be a garbage man. Some of us over here think of you English as professional eccentrics. With us there's maybe six or seven million trout fishermen. We start them on salmon roe or spinner. Then we start plugging the fly. Every magazine plugs it. It's fashionable. It's difficult. More beautiful. Easier to bait with salmon roe but more difficult to cast a fly. The difficulty of doing it is what attracts, that and the fashion.

There are private fishing clubs but they don't own the water, you cannot buy and sell these rivers, they own the surrounding land. If the water is not navigable you cannot get to it across the land without the permission of the owner. The land, as they say, is posted. Most of the clubs concentrate on the dry fly. I talked to one of these club members.

Fifteen years ago the idea of fishing the dry fly caught fire. We'd always fished it, some of us, since Theodore Gordon, but it's now really taken off. I think it's due to the professional propagandists in the fishing magazines and fishing books. I fished with Ed Hewitt. He was a bloody bore but he was a great promoter of the dry fly.

117

You have to take a breath to cope with everything you see and hear and are told. You have to learn new words – jassids and hoppers and tricos – and you have to learn new ways of fishing the fly and new ways to wade trout rivers that are double the size of Tweed and Tay put together, and sometimes you will fish from canoes, sometimes fly by floatplane for half a day or more to get to the river you want to fish. You are in a continent and the sheer size of everything takes some getting used to. Perhaps the most astonishing thing of all: you will be able to fish some of the finest trout water in the world for a week, or a month, or longer, merely for the cost of a state licence. Maybe twenty or thirty dollars. About the same as the price of a boat on Rutland Water for a day.

THEODORE GORDON'S fly box is on the mantelpiece, Halford's flies are in a nearby cupboard, on the walls is a Bateman cartoon, and in the bookshelves are first editions of fishing books by Edward Grey and Plunket Greene and a very early edition of Walton's *Compleat Angler*. You are not in London but four thousand miles away in the library and lunch room of the Anglers' Club of New York.

I think there must be some kind of freemasonry among fishermen, especially fly fishermen, which makes the transition from Europe to America comparatively easy, even more so if you happen to have the same background, have read the same books, and have a common bond in the same language, or what is, on the whole, still more or less the same language.

I like the Anglers' Club. It is a small building, not more than two storeys, but is surrounded and overshadowed by the enormous fifty-storey skyscrapers of downtown Manhattan and Wall Street. You would think they would dwarf it. They don't. The club is bright and gay and human-sized, with flags flying outside, windows overlooking the waters of the East River and Battery Point, and seeming to hold itself up with pride, conscious of history. Next door, indeed part of the same building, is the Fraunces tavern where George Washington gave a farewell celebratory dinner to his officers after the defeat of Cornwallis at Yorktown in 1781. That battle marked the end of British rule and the true foundation of the United States.

It was pleasant to discuss these things with our hosts, a lawyer, a business man, a doctor, in a lunch room which is as alike as two peas with the long dining room of the Garrick Club in London. There was a two-way play of ideas, a comforting sense that we were amused by the same things, that we had a strong sense of identity, especially when we dropped politics and history for the more important subject of fishing. The New York lawyer knew not only the Spey at Arndilly but the origin of that great salmon fly, the Arndilly Fancy, and exactly how it should be dressed. I was able to explain why that great American trout fly, the Adams, was so invaluable on the Hampshire chalk streams. So we went on and time flew by. After a lunch that must have lasted a good three hours we decided, reluctantly, that it was time to go.

The New York lawyer, saying goodbye to me at the door, reverted to our original discussions about Cornwallis and Washington. He grinned at me.

'Nice to have you Brits back here again.'

Fly in the sky

IT is said that under certain conditions of light, loch trout will not rise to a fly. The conditions are not always exactly similar but near enough to suggest a connection. In general, it is when the sky is overcast, the mist is low, and the water has a slightly metallic look. Halford described it as being

> . . . when the entire hemisphere of the sky is of one heavy, grey, dull, leaden colour, when the very light itself seems to have become imbued with this sad leaden tinge . . .

And one perhaps should add that in such conditions there generally seems to be very little wind.

But neither Halford nor anyone I know could explain why air conditions can affect trout and sea trout which are lying several feet below the surface of the water. They are certainly able to see a fly moving above them, whatever the light. They can even see them at night. So it must be something else, unless of course it's an old wives' tale. I doubt that. It seems to be almost universally accepted by ghillies with long experience that in certain lights the trout will not rise.

All Halford could suggest was that these light conditions preceded a change of weather and the fish did not like change. Later writers have suggested that changes in air pressure do affect the water. That would presumably mean that if the oxygen content of the water was low, or in the process of being lowered, the fish, being sensitive to the change, even though they may be some feet below the surface, would go off their feed. I am not scientist enough, or ichthyologist enough, to say whether this is so or not. The verdict must be 'not proven'. It is of course an excellent excuse for a blank day.

All the same, some very odd things do happen on stillwaters, not small lakes but big expanses of water of many hundreds of acres. I may be imagining it, but they seem to have an atmospheric chemistry of their own which is subtly different from that on or over the land. Take the case of the flying lines at Chew Valley lake.

The story was told to me by a fellow member of the Flyfishers' Club. He and a friend were fishing Chew Valley on the drift and the fishing was good. Then, a rather thick mist began to settle down quite close to the water, a kind of atmospheric condition they had not seen before. The mist was quite thick above the boat. In front of them it was as though the air and water were meeting. Everything became a kind of brownish-grey colour and they could no longer see the end of their lines when they were casting ahead.

They were drifting slowly over that part of the lake known as the Roman Shallows and through the mist they could see flickers of lightning on the hills around. Then the mist became thicker. One man, who was using a carbon fibre rod, suddenly found that something odd was happening to his line when he was casting. Instead of going out over the water it went up into the air and stayed there. They could see the line going right up into the overcast. Shortly afterwards the other man, who was using a glass fibre rod, found the same thing was happening to him.

There they were in the boat with their lines going up into the air.

Fishing was impossible for about half an hour. The flies simply would not go down on to the water. They sat there in the boat, curious, not particularly afraid in spite of the electrical disturbance, discussing various theories of static electricity, fields of force, and so on. Gradually the mist began to clear, things got better, and they could fish normally again.

I know of only one other case. I am grateful to Dr D. K. Black of Stourport on Severn for the following information about what happened when he and his wife and daughter were boat fishing on Loch Leven on August 24, 1956:

> I have kept a record of fishing days all my life and on the day in question the weather was very dull and it rained on and off all day. In the afternoon when we were on the far side of Castle Island I began to notice that my cast was becoming increasingly reluctant to settle on the water and eventually just seemed to hang in the air a foot or so above the surface. This lasted for some half to three-quarters of an hour or so.
>
> It was somewhat thundery and at the north end of the lake we saw what we took to be the beginnings of a waterspout, though it never came to anything. All this was very puzzling, and as I had never experienced its like before, I recounted it all to the man in the office when I went to weigh in our fish, for we had three trout that day, of a total weight of four pounds. However, the man just smiled and assured me it was nothing new. He gave it a name, but I cannot remember what it was. I expect you will have had plenty of explanations concerning electro-magnetic surface fields, which I am sure is the answer.

Fly in the sky

I ALWAYS remember the first fish that came to my fly. It was a chub of well over a pound and a half. I was only about nine or ten years old at the time and it was, to me, an enormous fish, bigger than anything I'd ever seen in the river and it came for me as I was lifting the fly from the surface of the water to cast again. The momentum of the fish going for the fly and the momentum of lifting off the line combined with an involuntary reaction on my part was sufficient to send fly and line and fish all together hurtling over my head without a pause. The fish fell in the grass and I fell on the fish. On the advice of my father, it was returned to the water. I always remember the mixture of regret and pleasure at the sight of it swimming away.

The trouble about learning to fish in those days half a century ago was that no one was really able to teach you how to cast. You watched someone, or someone gave you advice, and then you went away and tried to imitate what you had seen, or follow the rather hazy advice you were given. People had the impression that you picked up casting a fly as you went along. They did not have that impression about golf – for that you had to go to a professional for lessons – but they did about fishing. It took many years before it was generally accepted that to cast reasonably well, and certainly to get any distance, you needed an instructor for fly fishing just as much as you did in golf.

My father belonged to the old school and fishing the drift on a lake, or casting a short line to a trout on one of the Yorkshire becks, did not call for much skill in the use of the rod, a delicate flick and that was about all.

So I came to Blagdon and that was fine and easy on the drift but when I had to fish from the bank and needed to throw a long line I was in trouble. I can still remember the terrible sense of humiliation and inadequacy I suffered. I would not fish near anyone else in case they looked across at me and saw how badly I was casting. Months of struggle lay ahead, months of trying to cast this way or that way, as I imagined other people were doing it.

How jealous I was, how infuriated at the sight of one or two of the fishermen at Blagdon who made thier lines float out over the air for what seemed to be enormous distances without any apparent stress or strain. I struggled on, trying to copy their actions, always failing, and not understanding why I failed. A qualified instructor could have told me why in five minutes. I had to find out for myself and though it may not have taken five years it felt like it.

I am not sure what line velocity one gets from a good spring of the rod, some say it may be as much as eighty or a hundred miles an hour, or even more, and all these things can be worked out, no doubt, but for myself I am content with a fairly moderate speed which will let me cast about the length of a cricket pitch with a single-handed rod, so that I can cover most of a lake's marginal rises.

I came late to salmon and double-handed rods. It was not so bad with an overhead cast but I doubt whether anyone can learn to do a good Spey cast without an instructor. It is the same as getting a good swing at golf. You need the professional beside you saying do this, the arm so, lift here, now this, now that, and gradually you get the feel of it.

It is on the big salmon rivers that you do need to put out a long line, and that I know makes all the difference, for you must be able to cover the lies and they always seem to be far away by the opposite bank, and when you have a river with a fast flow that is maybe eighty yards wide, you will know what I mean. Deep wading and a long line is often the only way.

The smaller rivers are a good deal easier and I always remember that my very first salmon on the fly, taken on the Somerley water of the Hampshire Avon, came to one of the most horrible casts I have ever made. I was using a double-handed rod and a floating line and did something very odd in mid-air, so that the line fell in coils on the water with the fly in the middle of them. I was most embarrassed by the sight and was about to lift off to do a decent cast when a great salmon came up, shouldered its way through the coils of line, picked out the fly from the middle and swam off with it.

He was a big fish, twenty pounds plus I should imagine from the sight of him, and the powerful way he went off downstream, so that I had to chase him along the bank. He took all my line and most of the backing so I had to run fast and far to try and turn him. I never did. There was a ditch in my way; the mud looked solid, but wasn't and I went into it at speed. When I crawled out and sorted myself out the salmon had broken me and the ditch had broken a cartilage. It took me a good hour to hobble back to my car in the next field. However, I was in one way happy. I had learned another lesson.

It is not always the best cast that takes the best fish.

I AM grateful to those expert stillwater fishing writers who provide what I can best describe as insect tables in their fishing books. These tables tell you the months when the main stillwater insects will be hatching so that you can, with confidence, fish an imitative pattern at those times and know that you are doing the right thing. It must be a corixae month because the tables tell you it is, and so you fish a corixa pattern. All very simple and highly efficient and scientific. However, in my own admittedly limited experience, the trout do not take a great deal of notice of insect tables. There are even times when one suspects the trout ignore them.

That is the trouble. Insect tables are somehow a little remote from the reality of lake or reservoir. Great waves crash on the shore, strong winds sweep some bedraggled flying creature past, either too far away or too fast to be recognised for what it is. We make a wild guess at a sedge or an olive only to discover, from thumbing through the tables, that neither should be there because neither is in season. Therefore it must have been a midge, but it didn't look like one. Uncertainty leaves us in an imitative limbo.

This is where wet fly men and lure fishermen have the advantage. They put on a fly they like the look of and expect the trout to like the look of it too, and if the trout doesn't like it, they'll put on something else. I knew a man once who always started with a Greenwell and was quite prepared to follow it with his next favourite, a Mallard and Claret, but rarely had to change because the Greenwell generally did the trick after an hour or so. He took the line that the trout never read insect tables and there was therefore no reason why he should do so. He was a happy man, and he caught a reasonable number of fish, and he was quite willing to experiment from time to time. Next season he thought he might well begin with a Connemara Black and see if that did as well as the Greenwell. He was doubtful if it would, but there was no harm in trying.

All goes well with this kind of approach providing the fisherman fishes with the flies that he likes the look of and hopes that sooner or later a trout will feel the same. That's fine. But as soon as the wet fly man starts to think of his flies from the trout's point of view he gets into the same state of uncertainty as the imitative fisherman who has got confused about his corixae. Is this the best time of the month for the Connemara, he will say to himself, peering into his box, or perhaps a Kingfisher Butcher might do better in July?

Uncertainty, however, is no handicap. It is a decided advantage. Doubts over the choice of fly and our ignorance of the tastes and habits of trout add tremendously to our pleasure. If the success of our fly patterns were in any way predictable, a large part of our enjoyment in fishing a fly would disappear. It would be no more exhilarating than throwing a seine net or dragging a beam trawl. All we would be concerned with, if that happened, would be the catch.

THE choice of fly does become a little complex, particularly for beginners. Dry flies are an understandable source of confusion. It would be a little easier if a dry fly that was tied to suggest the large dark olive was marketed as a large dark olive, but as it is there are maybe half a dozen artificial patterns, all with different names, which, with variations, represent that one natural insect. There is the Greenwell, the Blue Upright, Kite's Imperial and the Beacon Beige for a start, and no doubt others. All can represent a large dark olive.

The way round it for a beginner is to ignore names, and to go through the trays of dry flies in the tackle shop and make his own particular choice from size and shape and colour. He will pick out a sedge or two and some small Black Gnats and that will be fairly easy. But now come the olives and a vast choice is before him. He should pick out a few large and a few small olive duns, some of a dark shade and some a light shade and a couple of spinners, and only later need he bother about what they are called. They will be good enough for most of the streams he is likely to fish, in southern England at least, together with a few seasonal variations, such as the big mayfly and the crane fly.

For the spate rivers of the north and west he will find good advice in most of the local tackle shops, for their owners will generally be fishermen themselves and anxious to help. A Blue Upright and a Coachman will do for a good deal of the dry fly work in Devon. For Yorkshire and the Borders the beginner must be initiated into the mysteries of the Partridge and Orange, Dun Spiders and Poult Bloas. On the great rivers of the Dales he will not worry too much about the dry fly and matching the hatch, nor will he on the Borders.

He should be encouraged to take a light-hearted view of his choice of fly, not considering it in a serious way as if he was buying an equity, but more like taking a ticket in a lottery. He should be at all costs disabused of the idea, that seems to be extraordinarily prevalent among beginners, that there is such a thing as a right choice of fly. There are certain times when one guesses right and other times, which are more frequent, when one guesses wrong. He must also be warned that if one pattern of fly happens to be successful on one day it will almost invariably be unsuccessful on the next. In this way he will be able to prepare himself for the fly fisherman's proper state of mind: an exhilarating and deliciously bemused uncertainty.

IF you want to see a really fine choice of flies, examine a reservoir fisherman. At one time it used to be salmon fishermen. But not now. Reservoir fishermen carry flies in a portmanteau, tray upon tray upon tray, all shapes and colours and sizes: five-inch double-hooked lures, full of fluff and colour; jolly-looking jigs with beady eyes; popper bugs and wagglers; and then more trays of imitation worms and nymphs and pupae in sober lines; then back to the brightness of Butchers and Dunkelds, the old traditional wetflies; and finally – and this is the mark of the man who ties his own flies – a fairly nondescript collection of patterns which do not appear to fit into any category unless it is akin to what might be called spiders.

These stillwater spiders are interesting. They have a long pedigree, deriving from some of the loch patterns fished by R. C. Bridgett, the Glasgow schoolmaster, not far off a hundred years ago, and from the Border spiders of Stewart, which puts them back a couple of hundred years or more. In fact some of the spiders I saw fished only the other day at a Hampshire lake are similar to Stewart's, only larger and with a weighted underbody of lead or copper wire. That apart, they carry out the same function as Stewart's spiders: to create the illusion of life.

The dressing is simple, which is another advantage. The body is of floss silk or nylon or fine wool over the weighted underbody which is tapered towards the bend of the hook. There are no whisks. At the head of the fly are three or four turns of a speckled hackle, like a partridge, or a plain hackle, the fibres swept well back over the body. The fly is tied in four or five different plain colours which include brown, claret, green and yellow, and of course a black. Some dressers put on a fine wire rib but this seems to be optional. The black looks well with it; with the coloured flies it is barely visible.

These spider patterns have given rise in recent years to what might be called the impressionist school of stillwater fly dressing. A rather pompous description which merely means that the aim of the dressing is to create an impression of life without any direct attempt at imitation, a form of conjuring trick, the creation of illusions.

IN a neat white glass-fronted picture frame in one of the rooms of the Flyfishers' Club in London is a collection of maggots. They are technically not maggots, which are the larvae of blowflies, but their underwater equivalents, the larvae and pupae of midges and sedges. They are not the real thing either but imitations tied on hooks, quite small hooks, maggot size.

They are historic imitation maggots – cod-bait was the old name for some of them – for these were the first imitation bait patterns tied for stillwater fishing by Dr Howard Alexander Bell of Blagdon, in the 19͡ ͡ , which led to the development of what we now call, incorrectly but as a matter of convenience, stillwater nymph fishing.

Bell, influenced by Skues, spooned out the stomach contents of the trout he caught at Blagdon and tied imitations of the creatures he found there. He fished his imitation larvae and pupae flies three to a cast, mostly on a greased line, using the knot at the end of the line as a bite-indicator. He wandered along looking for rising fish, exploring weed beds and wide fertile shallows. Bell's Bush at the top end of Blagdon is his memorial. He wrote nothing, shunned publicity, and when someone showed him an article which had been written about his methods in *The Field* he tore it up.

A strange man, yet without much doubt the father of imitative bait fishing on stillwaters. He was the first to tie the Blagdon Buzzer, the Grenadier, and the Amber Nymph, though he

129

would certainly not recognise the modern tyings as being in any way related to his own, except by name. His were very thin, they had a meagre covering of floss on the hook, or a single strand of wool, with a fine wire rib, hardly any head to speak of and sometimes, though not always, half a dozen short hackle fibres, sloping well back.

My grandfather, Willie Cox, was by no means alone in disliking the appearance of Bell's baits. Functional, yes, and very deadly at times, for they follow the principle of imitating the creatures on which the trout are feeding or are expected to feed, so there is no argument about that at all. I have fished them myself at Blagdon and at certain times, during the evening rise, I would never fish anything else if I wanted to take a trout, so there is no argument about that either. And yet, I do not like thee, Dr Bell, though I am not at all sure why.

Possibly it is Willie Cox, surviving in me, who gives me a mild unease at the sight of Dr Bell's baits. I look at them with a certain distaste, a feeling of disapproval. It is nothing to do with whether or not they are efficient. They are highly efficient. It is something else, and whether it is to do with a sense of propriety, with an aesthetic sense, I do not know, but I suspect it may be that I like to fish with a fly that gives me pleasure not only to tie but to look at. Maggoty flies, bait flies, for some reason, perhaps a puritanical upbringing, bring me no pleasure.

I suspect that since Dr Bell quite a few fishermen and fly designers have attempted, subtly no doubt, to restore the balance. They have taken the basic maggoty fly and put in a touch of colour here and there, a little wisp of something on the top, a bit of fluff (only a touch you understand) on the tail, so that the overall appearance is less spartan, a little more elegant than the original. Fly fishing is not only a matter of magic, of creating illusions, but of creating elegant illusions. The fly must take fish, oh, indeed, that is its function, but at the same time, if it can attract fishermen as well it is much more likely to be used and to survive.

BUYING a new fly rod is not to be entered into lightly. It needs thought. Although emotionally one may long for a new and beautiful rod that does everything the catalogues may say about it, and they say a great deal, it also needs a fairly sober assessment on how the fisherman and the rod are going to get on together. On this point, although the analogy may be a little stretched, the choice of a rod has some affinity with a marriage. One hopes it will last for some time.

Matching a rod to a fisherman is by no means an easy matter; the shape of the handle, even the colour of the whipping may be as important, or nearly so, as the movement and flex of the rod itself. I knew a man once who refused to buy a rod he liked because the word *carbon* and the maker's name were inscribed in large lettering on the butt just above the handle. The lettering, he said, was far too large and he did not like going fishing carrying advertisements.

To others, however, the carrying of advertisements may be as much a matter of pride as a blazon in heraldry is of its owner's rank and quality, for a fisherman whose clothing and tackle are ornamented with a myriad badges and names and trophies is at least proclaiming to the world that he is a man of substance and experience, and by no means to be regarded as a beginner or a novice in his affairs. It is very much a matter of personal taste.

And this, of course, is the key to the choice of rod, for two rods by the same maker of almost identical size and shape may well feel very different when casting a line. Even on the same bench, production methods with composite materials can vary. Certainly a few inches either way in the length of a rod, or the fraction of a millimetre in its tapers, can make all the difference to the feel of it when it is moving under the hand with the pressure of a line. Such things have a subtle appeal that will only be discovered in use and are unlikely to be judged correctly from advertisements in catalogues and magazines. There is nothing so good as seeing and feeling what it is you are going to buy.

It is also true that there is nothing so good as a rod which is beautifully finished and gives one pleasure to look at. I have used cheap rods, one which was functional enough but poorly finished, and one which had a reasonable finish but was made of a poor-quality blank which ultimately broke on the slightest of snags, and neither gave much pleasure in use. On the other hand, a rod I knew I could not afford to buy but did so has given me considerable pleasure for many years. One suspects that rods which have become good companions, have shared in frustrations, have helped one to triumphs, are not to be accounted in terms other than that of friends; and friendship is not to be judged by cost.

Vice and vises

THE traditional English fisherman must be forgiven if he looks a little askance at the latest American invention: an automated fly-tying vice. It is called, in America, a vise. Details are given in the American magazine, *Fly Tier*.

The fly-tying machine to some extent looks like an ordinary vice (vise) except for the cables and plugs and things that are necessary for its operation. The advertisement tells us that it can hold hooks from size 6 through 22 and

    . . . is driven by a motor with a full power variable speed

control specially designed for this vise. There's also an on/off button that stops the vise spinning immediately, with no coasting when released.

It is reassuring to know that the vice does not coast when released. The thought of a size 22 midge in the jaws of the vice revolving at speed while a full-power drive rips silk off the bobbin at several thousand revs a minute as the machine coasts to a halt could make prospective customers a little anxious. The makers clearly have had this in mind. Indeed, they seem, with typical American efficiency, to have thought of everything. Not only do they suggest you buy an all-electric vice (vise) for yourself but you should

. . . order one now for that special friend or loved one. It works great.

Some might feel, however, that not all our loved ones are interested in vice (vise), particularly all-electric vices, even if they do work great. Probably they would not wish to work them at all even if they have mastered the technique of the full power variable speed control, and − knowing our loved ones − would probably object to a gift which would come with the implication that they ought to run off a couple of dozen duns before breakfast.

On the whole, it might be a good thing to have second thoughts about buying more than one of these machines until it is quite clear whether it is worth while spending a large number of dollars not only on our loved ones but on our special friends. Moreover, knowing what most of our fly tying is like, does the machine, as it were, go far enough?

For a nation that can send men to the moon and circle the globe in sixty seconds (or whatever the current rate may be), they should not have all that difficulty in knocking up a machine that will make the hand-tied fly entirely a thing of the past, taking in hooks and fur and feathers at one end and ejecting the finished flies at several hundred flies a second at the other.

In that case, however, deprived of our ordinary vices (vises) what would we find to do during the long winter evenings with our special friends?

TYING flies in the traditional way is a very pleasant hobby, rather like needlework, and there is nothing so satisfying as taking a fish on a fly you have tied yourself; but one must be careful not to become too involved. A couple of Greenwells, or something of that kind, when required, is reasonable enough, providing one puts away the clutter of fur and feather and bits of cotton afterwards that have been discarded and not leave them lying about all over the sitting-room. The danger sign is when the fly-tyer tells his family that he must have a room of his own in which to exercise his hobby. That is the break point. A sure sign of addiction.

If the family gives way, as may happen, and an attic or something of that kind is put at his disposal, they will see little of him from then on, for a man who is passionately involved in creating perfect copies of Baetis (or attempting to do so, for he will be unlikely to succeed) has very little thought for his wife and children. By the time he has stayed up past midnight wrestling with his latest design of the Blue-winged Olive, his wife will be in bed and fast asleep. It will be too late to make amends.

A subtle change of character often takes over. A certain ruthlessness becomes apparent. He will think nothing of clipping his wife's fur coat, if she has one, or shaving the family cat to acquire the materials of his craft. In this he merely follows the example of past masters of the art of fly dressing, men like R. S. Austin of Tiverton who clipped urine-stained fur from the private parts of a ram to get the right body-colour for the Tups. Incidentally it may be wondered whether the ram permitted Austin to do so without reprisals. Rams in North Devon are not the most likely of animals to give up their private parts for clipping by comparative strangers without a struggle.

Not that danger would deter the real addict from scavenging any animal in sight whose hair is sufficiently desirable. No bird, from peacocks to the ordinary domestic fowl, is safe but he will have both tail and cape. Gradually his collection spreads from box to box, from room to room, until the whole house is pervaded by the smell of anti-moth powder and decaying skins. At this stage there is no known cure.

THE tedium of fixed spool spinning has been largely overcome by the Monagasques.

They have invented a machine which does it for you. A self-propelled artificial bait is attached to a rod and line and placed in the water. On that instant, so we are assured, it takes off and buzzes round the lake – *buzz, buzz* – entirely on its own until it is taken by a fish. It is said in the newspaper advertisements to be infallible as a means of catching big *brochets* and *grosse truites*.

The Leurre Auto-Propulse, about the size of an American plug, perhaps a little larger, is marketed by the Gloria Corporation of Monaco, and may be had by readers of *France Dimanche* at a bargain price of 34.50 francs which includes a recharge of carburant. What happens to readers of other newspapers who want a recharge is not clear.

The Leurre will no doubt save the user from the old-fashioned method of casting his plug or spoon every few minutes or so, but on the other hand there may be problems about which we are not told. When a pike or trout takes the Leurre, does it stop buzzing, or is the carburant so strong that the thing continues to charge round the lake dragging the poor fish with it? How often does it need to be recharged and is it a nice clean quick business or a messy spooning of some sticky substance into a combustion chamber?

However, there is no doubt about the ingenuity of the Gloria

Corporation of Monaco. Not only have they achieved a first with their self-propelled plug, they have invented and marketed an automatic hooker. This also is available to readers of *France Dimanche* at the bargain price of 44.50 francs and no doubt a bargain it is, especially for those middle-aged fishermen one sees on the banks of the Seine in Paris who are inclined to drop off for a while after a heavy lunch. The automatic hooker, Le Bouchon Ferreur it is called, will hook a fish for them and wake them up into the bargain.

From the drawing of the Bouchon in the advertisement, it seems to be a rather large float or pike-bung and inside it is a clockwork spring. When a fish takes the bait it pulls on the spring, the spring pulls back, hooks the fish, and at the same time makes a loud noise, illustrated by the advertisement artist with the word *Clac!* which he illustrates as being surrounded by vibrations that indicate the volume of noise the Bouchon can produce.

Most ingenious, of course, especially for the elderly and comatose. No longer is there any need to watch that little quill for hour after hour as it rides the ripples, circled with red and white and green, bobbing a little, trembling at times, lying flat, sliding away, the sudden dip and tilt as it flickers under the surface and leviathan moves below. All this uncertainty is removed at one loud *Clac!* The fisherman of the age of the automata needs merely to set the spring, bait the hook, put up the deckchair and umbrella and read the paper. It may be very pleasant but all the same one cannot keep feeling it is not quite what fishing ought to be about.

A HUNDRED and fifty years ago, or thereabouts, a professional fly-dresser and ghillie, James Wright, who lived and had his business at Bowden Cottage in Sprouston, a village on the banks of the Tweed near Kelso, defied all the conventions of his time and clipped a plume of hair from the tail of the vicar's dog and created what we now believe to have been the first hairwing salmon fly, the Garry Dog. The date this happened is unknown, but it was probably around 1850. Authentication is lacking, nevertheless this is as near as one can get.

There is a name of Wright in the graveyard, another on Sprouston war memorial, but all other family records seem to have gone; the dog which was cropped for his plumes was buried by the footpath between Sprouston and the Butterwash, but the headstone is no longer there and one account says it is now somewhere in Gateshead-on-Tyne. These are about the only scraps of information that are left to us, infuriatingly scanty and often contradictory.

Wright's place in fly-fishing history is nevertheless assured, for in addition to his hairwing salmon flies – setting a dog to catch a salmon, as someone said – he has to his credit the Greenwell's Glory, the Durham Ranger, Silver Grey, and Thunder and Lightning. One or two of these dressings might be challenged, but the Garry and the Greenwell are securely his, even if Canon Greenwell played a part in instructing Wright as to what kind of dressing might be best.

The only challenger to the Garry as the first hairwing might well be the Hairy Mary which was presumably first dressed from some unknown Mary's hair, but the origin is obscure, perhaps deliberately so to spare the poor girl's feelings. There are a number of questions of this kind which deserve to be answered, though it is unlikely that they will be. Was the dog named Garry a retriever, a Labrador, and were his plumes used in their natural colour or dyed? Wright was a professional dresser and certainly would know the use of dyes. Bright colours would be in demand for the heavily coloured waters of the Tweed in autumn. But, alas, the more fly-dressers of today probe into the past the less certainty there is.

The sea trout

SILVER flashes in the shallows, vee shapes arrowing upwards into the flow, a fin breaking the surface, a sense of urgency and tension communicated to the watchers on the bank above, and the annual miracle of the sea trout's river run has begun.

Sea trout look uncommonly like salmon and from the time of the game laws onwards for many hundreds of years were thought of as salmon, and why not? Yet every now and again observant men saw that there were slight differences. The eyes were not in the same place as those of a salmon, nor was the tail forked.

No one can be certain when it was, but around a hundred or a hundred and fifty years ago we knew the truth: that the sea trout was a migratory brown trout which had changed its size and shape and colouring because of its sea-going habits. So fishmongers, who had always thought of them as salmon, now had to call them salmon trout.

Regional names were another matter. There must be a dozen

or more apart from the well-known ones – sewin in Wales, finnock and herling in Scotland, peal in Devon, and white trout in Ireland – but these seem more and more applied to maiden fish, those small fish which come up the rivers in shoals around harvest and hay-making times – and which Devon fishermen call harvest peal. But the large fish, anything over four pounds up to about twenty – which is about as large as they come – are given their proper name, sea trout. The official British record sea trout weighed exactly twenty pounds and was caught in 1983 by a Mr G. Leavy who took it in the Castle Pool on the Tweed.

Establishing an official record is not quite so easy as one might imagine. Far more is needed than hanging the fish on a spring balance from the fishing bag and getting it witnessed. The fish itself has to be laid upon the table of a body of experts in Peterborough known as the British Record (Rod-Caught) Fish Committee.

Mr Leavy's twenty-pound fish was no doubt sent to Peterborough as fast as British Rail could manage and there underwent several intensive examinations, including one which was described by *The Field* as electrophoretic tests. This, *The Field* must have felt, was a phrase that would satisfy everyone that the inquest on Mr Leavy's fish was being carried out in a thoroughly scientific way so they did not consider it necessary to explain what electrophoretic tests were. One puts aside as unworthy the suspicion that they might not have known.

According to *Chambers Dictionary*, electrophoretic pertains to electrophoresis, from the Greek *phoresin*, meaning to bear, and that electrophoresis involves the migration of suspended particles as protein macro-molecules under the influence of an electric field. One assumes that in some darkened room of the British Record (Rod-Caught) Fish Committee men in white coats applied electric fields of a stupendous power to Mr Leavy's sea trout in order to migrate its suspended particles.

Caution is of course always justified, especially in a committee that deals with fish. Ever since the story of Jonah and the Whale, fishermen's stories have become notorious for exaggeration, often unjustly no doubt, but in view of the general opinion on the subject the fish had to be produced and laid upon the slab. So far so good. What may be a little more doubtful is whether it was necessary to interfere with its macro-molecules.

Scientists move in a mysterious way which a mere angler finds incomprehensible. Why – he might well ask – is it necessary to electrocute a sea trout in order to establish it as a record and what is likely to happen to the fish when its suspended particles are migrated, and for that matter where do they migrate to?

And what happens to a fish after its electrophoretic tests have been concluded? Is it still eatable after its particles have been moved, or is it even recognisable as a fish at all? It would indeed be sad if a record sea trout were to end up as unrecognisable protein in the waste disposal bins of the Peterborough laboratories. The scientists ought to tell us, otherwise the next fisherman who catches what he hopes is a bigger sea trout might be tempted to avoid such unknown mutilations and try the *Guinness Book of Records* instead.

THE best thing to do to welcome the opening of the sea trout season is to have a party, a small party – nothing elaborate because that would be out of place – but a small dinner party with two intimate old friends, and your wife and yourself, all fishers, all ready to go down to the river at dusk.

One would start, if I might make a suggestion, with a good fino sherry or a malt whisky, which would be followed by something cooked in advance, like a shepherd's pie, ready waiting in the oven, rich and spicy and with a crisp brown crust. Nothing after that, except fruit or cheese, but an especially good red wine to go with the shepherd's pie would be important. A feast of this calibre needs good conversation to go with it, such as whether one is to use large or small flies, and whether one can manage a couple of droppers in the dark. There will be a great deal of quotation, or misquotation, from fishing

141

textbooks to prove something that will seem important at the time.

In good heart, but not too full of food and wine to make life lie heavy, it will be time for departure. Along the road, park the car in the layby, and down over the field to where the river lies hidden under a screen of trees. The cows in the field are asleep and will hardly move for your passing. It is dusk and bats are already at work. Owls will be around later. Everything is soft and quiet and hushed so that the slightest noise will have you looking back over your shoulder to see who is following. But, for the moment, you are fortified by good companions and the night's rustling fears are at a distance.

Not all will go smoothly. Time will be spent on such things as getting hooks out of woollen sweaters and investigating why the torch, which had a new battery only that afternoon, now works intermittently or not at all. There will be doubts whether you have put your friends on the best pools, and mishaps such as falling over rocks, slipping on mud, getting tackle hung up in bushes, and tearing waders on wayward strands of wire. Perhaps you will avoid most of them, though hazards do seem to lie in wait, especially when your mind is on other things and you have just heard a sea trout rise.

Rise is perhaps the wrong word. The noise is more like a brick being thrown into the water, an angry and rather bullying sound as the fish leaps clear of the surface and crashes down again, making what we used to call as small boys in our swimming pool a real belly-flopper. Whether the fish are angry, or just plain bored, or suffering from some other inexplicable fishy emotion, which humans would have difficulty in understanding, is difficult to say. Whatever the reason, the fish has betrayed itself. There, where you saw the flash of white water, is where you put the fly.

But you yourself may be betrayed by too much haste. In this half-darkness, if you move too fast to get into position, especially if you have to wade, you will find the trout have good guardians, algae-covered sloping rocks and ledges that mask treacherous pools. A wading stick helps at times but above all else it is necessary to hasten slowly. Here, and throughout the night, it seems right to regard yourself as being in enemy territory and to behave accordingly.

The charm of night fishing does lie to a great extent in this element of danger. There will be times when, quite suddenly and unexpectedly, the danger will seem very real, even if it is only something rustling in the undergrowth followed by the crash of a startled deer. These are moments when it is good to have a companion. It is much more of a festival, a celebration, when one goes fishing with friends.

It is best, too, to come back together at some reasonable time, so that one can weigh the fish, if there are any, or commiserate with each other if there are not, and sit around the kitchen table telling tales of the ones that got away and how this was done and that happened, drinking cups of hot chocolate, perhaps followed by more whisky before bed.

What splendid expeditions these can be!

EDWARD GREY once wrote that sea trout were fish without a home, and this is true, a gipsy fish they are, always on the move, travelling up river, travelling down, off and away and out to sea. At times, when they have come into the river on their way to spawn, they can be curiously uncertain about themselves and where they're going.

A shoal, newly in the river, will sometimes turn and follow a leader downstream for a little way, then turn and wander back again, not necessarily to the place from which they came but to some other, which they did not appear to choose but simply stopped there because they did not know what else to do.

Suddenly something happens. Maybe a freshet of water comes

which is invisible to the watching fisherman, for the river may not rise an inch; but something has come, a taste, a coldness, something stimulating, an exhilarating draught of bubbling oxygen, instead of the tepid water they have been breathing, and in a flash they are changed and filled with purpose. If they had forgotten where they were going, or why, they have forgotten no longer. They are revived and vigorous, muscles taut, fins working, eager to seek the consummation that instinct promises awaits them on the gravel shallows of the moors.

The most civilised way of taking a sea trout is with a fly and some of the most exciting places to fish for them are the sea pools of the tiny burns of the west of Scotland and the Isles. The seas around Arran and Knapdale and the Mull of Kintyre have a vivid beauty and clarity which go back to the birth of the world. Litter is unknown, for the places you have to reach to find the sea-pools may never have been seen by another man for years, maybe a decade.

I had followed one burn in Knapdale for several hours, struggling through bracken and maiden pine, until I saw the glint of sea through the trees in front of me and came out into a glade so beautiful that it might have been the stage setting for a pastoral idyll. The pool was surrounded by carpets of moss and intricate grasses full of small wild flowers, and here and there were smooth granite boulders full of transparent specks which reflected the sunlight.

I sat down on one of the boulders to watch the pool. Far down in the crystal-clear water were thick green weeds, lifting and moving gently to the rhythm of the incoming tide, a movement that gave the illusion that this green covering was alive and breathing. There were no signs of fish.

I put a fly across the pool and there was a flash of silver from the weeds and a sea trout of a pound or more shot six or seven feet to the surface, took my fly, and fled with it back to cover. I was so surprised, I would have lost him if he had not hooked himself. What on earth brought up a good fish all that distance to take a tiny fly, a Peter Ross, no larger than a 12, or a 10 at the outside?

144

There is a nice ironmonger's shop in Tarbert, which stocks fishing tackle as well, where the owner will willingly discuss the necessity for small flies in sea-pools, and provide them, and a map as well to show you where the best pools are, for that is the kind of hospitality you get in that part of the world. We talked for some time but neither of us could be certain why a trout would rise so far to take a tiny speck of a fly just under the ripple.

One thing was, however, certain for both of us, that one should never try to take a fish of that quality on a worm or a metal spoon: it has to be a fly, and a good pattern, nothing with weight in it or bits of cork stuck on to it with Superglue, but a true fly along traditional lines, full of light and colour and sparkle. We had no idea why on the west coast and in the Western Isles there were so many small flies fished for the sea trout, and why on the east coast there were so many large, even very large ones, such as Terrors and Demons. We came to the conclusion it must be a matter of fashion.

It is surprising how sea trout flies come into and go out of fashion rapidly. In the 1950s one of the most popular sea trout tandems was the Dr Evelyn Sea-Trout Lure which was marketed, I remember, by Hardy's. Within ten years they vanished completely and in came Hugh Falkus's Sunk Lure, a tandem almost exactly the same as Evelyn's except it lacked the jungle cock cheeks and had blue streamers instead of red. I dislike tandems, especially for their capacity for foul hooking. I dislike trebles, because they are so difficult to remove from undersized fish, and I hold the fly-maggot in a mild contempt for being not all that far away from poaching.

SEA TROUT in lochs must get confused. Maybe that is why they circle around so much looking for a way out. Maybe that is why they take a fly on the dap. They have got bored. They have got nowhere. They want something to do. They have lost the river they thought was going to lead them to the spawning ground. It has led them to an inland sea. There may be no way out.

It is foolish to think in such terms. Entertaining though it may be to put words into their mouths, it does nothing to answer the mystery of what they are thinking, if indeed they can be said to think at all. It would be interesting if fishery scientists could tell us a bit more about the thinking of fish, though they would probably be reluctant to commit themselves to saying *thinking* at all, preferring something non-committal, like responses to stimuli.

Not so long ago a goodly number of biologists, zoologists and ichthyologists met in a seminar on the sea trout for three days in the Welsh mountains and one of the first questions that they asked, and one that recurred throughout the discussions, was: what are sea trout?

At first sight that might be regarded as an unnecessary question because we all know what sea trout are: biologically they belong to the same species as the brown trout, *Salmo trutta*, and that is that, they are the migratory version of the brown trout.

It is more complex. According to the scientists, in some rivers it is only the female sea trout that goes down to the sea while the male remains in the river. He will fertilise the females on their return. In the river, does he remain a sea trout if he takes on the colouration and habits of the brown? A nice point. A more complex one: there are specific genetic differences in sea trout that go back to the ice age. There appear to be two different types.

At this stage, not being scientists, we had better stop, but anyone interested can see the report of the seminar which is among those invaluable blue books published by the Atlantic Salmon Trust. It is, however, good to have if only a brief glimpse into what scientists are thinking, for it is a help in understanding some of the odd things that happen in sea trout fishing. Only recently I landed a sea trout of just under four pounds from a river in Mayo, in Ireland, which had almost

146

perfect brown trout markings. Yet it was taken only a mile or so above the tide, and was a male fish in excellent condition. Had he come from the sea? Had he come down from the lough to meet and escort the returning females? I have no answers. At least I have been able to phrase the questions.

Blue grass

Blue, blue is the grass beside the river

I USED to think that was imagining things, but coming up by the weir-pool the other day I saw what looked like a patch of blue grass on the stone slab by the fish-pass. Looking closer, it resolved itself into hundreds of thousands of dead elvers, all stiffened and entwined in death on that particular patch of stone from which the water had receded and the sun had broiled.

Just below the fish-pass, at the edge of the white water, were

148

the living ones, millions of them, the water black with elvers as far as I could see. How they were ever going to get up the fish-pass with its torrent of water I had no idea, but either they must have got up or gone round somehow, for the next week there was no sign of them, or of the blue grass.

It leaves one rather blank to consider the force that drives these tiny colourless strips of life so many thousands of miles from their deep-sea birth to our rivers and lakes. Fish have small brains, but those of an elver must be less in size than half a grain of sand. Fishermen are among those who are inclined to notice and to think of such things. Not that they understand them. The migration of elvers is not normally among the subjects they are prepared to discuss, even if they knew anything about it, which is unlikely. But they do have, as river keepers have, a sense of wonder at the world about them, which is not easily encouraged in a city. Not only fishermen have this sense. I remember a famous astronomer, Sir James Jeans, once saying that the more he knew of the universe, the more astonishing it became. Much the same can be said about fishermen and fishing. The more we experience, the less dogmatic we are likely to become, the more we accept that there is so little that we know.

It was certainly true in the case of the dancing stoat. I am not sure whether the stoat was actually dancing, as we know dancing, but that was what it appeared to be doing. We had been fishing in the Spey and had come back to the lodge; looking out of the big downstair windows we saw a stoat come running on to the lawn. In the middle of the lawn it suddenly leapt into the air, twisted round in mid-air, came down and ran a few paces in the other direction, then did another leap, a twist, and off in another direction. It continued to do this for some time, running, leaping and twisting, while we all watched in amazement. Then it ran down the drive and went off into the undergrowth.

When we told the ghillie about it he said it was probably doing this to hypnotise a rabbit. The only trouble about this explanation was that there was no sign of a rabbit. Someone thought it might have been a neurotic stoat imagining there was a rabbit somewhere. A simpler explanation could have been that it was a stoat that liked dancing.

Talking of hypnotising rabbits, a rabbit had a go at me only the previous year. I was walking along the river at a place on the Carron water known as The Sands and I came across a rabbit sitting in a sandy hollow a couple of yards or so in front of me. You would have thought that any self-respecting wild rabbit would have bolted like mad at the sight of man. This one didn't. It stared at me. I stared back. Then the odd thing happened. After a minute or so of staring I felt I was being hypnotised. I felt I would have difficulty in looking away. I made an effort, I did look away, and I walked past. The rabbit watched me go, turning his head to watch me, and I turned my head to watch him until we were out of sight of each other. He was not frightened. I could have reached out and touched him with my rod. How do you explain that rabbit?

OVER Loch Hope were seven eagles. A thousand feet up they were, maybe more, great birds with outstretched wings, soaring effortlessly around and around the empty sky in gliding rhythm, riding the air currents coming up the face of the mountain.

It was wonderful to see those great birds, a feeling of mutual interest went out from us towards them, a feeling of companionship. There they were, drifting the air, and here we were, drifting the loch, rods idle, staring, craning our necks, all of us wild creatures, hunting and playing.

We had been fishing the drift on Loch Hope, two boats out from Altnaharra, and from the moment we saw the eagles none of us fished. We watched for perhaps half an hour and then the birds began to drift away, around the peak, over to the other side, out of sight. We never saw them again. Two pairs, we thought, and their young, but at that distance it was impossible to be sure.

Here, in the far north, in the rocky crags and the river plains of Sutherland, time has stopped and the wilderness is all. By the side of the single-track road you will see a grey stone tower, a Pictish broch, which has been there a thousand years. Down in the valley the red deer graze by broken stones. There are ridges in the grass that might once have been places where men lived.

In Strathnaver, all around, are the remains of the Clearances, of the terror that began in 1814 when whole villages were destroyed, their houses and pastures burned, the people evicted so that the Sutherland land might be turned over to the grazing of sheep. One place above all is haunted, or it is to me, though there must be many others.

Take the road from Altnaharra, from the hotel, up through the little village, past the post office, and turn right at the cross-road along the road by Loch Naver. At the end of the loch, where the river begins, take a track to your right. When you reach the river, turn left, and you will come across a place of green fields in the midst of heather, and there are the heaps of stones that were once the village of Achness. The houses were burned over the heads of the people who lived there, people of the clan Mackay, who were turned out on to the hills in winter.

Those who survived the exposure and the lack of food found their way downriver to the seaside fishing village of Bettyhill and from there, some of them, the lucky ones, found passage to the American colonies. If you are a Mackay in the United States today, then as like as not you came from the clans that were evicted from Strathnaver.

Strathnaver, the valley of the river Naver, is a beautiful place, but it is also a place to remember for the Clearances and for the ill that was done to many thousands. At Achness there is as yet no memorial to that time, as there should be. Let us also give the names of some of the other villages that were destroyed in that valley: Mallart, Syre, Caenn-na-coille, Carnachadh, Skail, Rhiloisk, Achoul, Dalvina, and Dalharrold, which means Harrold's Field, a place that once

151

belonged to a Norseman. All have gone. So have the people. It is said that the Countess Elizabeth felt pity for them.

Pity did not stop the burning.

THE Irish, or some of them, still believe in the little people. That is not surprising. They have seen the dance of the mayflies. There is nothing quite like an Irish mayfly. A fairy creature with gauzy wings and a body of flame that dances in the sunset by the loughs and rivers. They are little people. There is no doubt.

Love affairs develop between man and fairy creatures. A friend of mine, David Jacques, fell in love with a sedge fly, the grannom:

> As the dove to Noah, the sea to Xenophon, or the shores of the homeland to the weary traveller, so is the first spring Grannom to the fly-fisher.

He bred them in a shed in his garden. He fed them on bread and chicken crumbs held out towards them on the point of a needle. He told the British Museum things about them that even the Museum didn't know. He contradicted Halford. He was at odds with Darwin. All from the grannom.

> For how can I fail to feel affection for this gentle insect in whose delectable company I have passed so many hours. From its very birth I watched it, clumsily and awkwardly, engaged in tumbling games with its brothers and sisters; then, through its infancy and maturity, nestling in its case, harming no other living creature but waiting patiently and trustingly for the victuals on which its life depends to be brought to its threshold; to its breathtaking metamorphosis from an aquatic animal to a fairy-like creature of the air, and, finally, to its lonely death in obscurity. All these things have I seen and to

me, if to none other, the Grannom will take its place alongside its more renowned contemporaries as one of the great flies of the fly-fisherman's world.

I don't see why we should not fall in love with a fly. Without flies we would have no fishing.

THE heron was standing motionless in the shallows. It was a young bird. You could tell that from the darkish plumage which looked like a dusty shawl draped round its shoulders. Maybe it was on its first outing from the heronry downstream, in the big wood, where the birds sit on their nests with their legs sticking through them and talk heron-talk to each other.

I don't know who taught the heron to fish. Possibly it is instinctive. There was not a flicker, not a movement, even the feathers tightened so they would not move in the wind. The head was poised in the position of the strike, the beak forward and down, head at an angle over the stream. It gave the impression that at any moment there would be a controlled power drive. You could feel the intentness, the concentration.

When movement of the body came it was elaborately, painstakingly slow. One leg was lifted gently from the water, toes coming together in the elegance of a dancer on points, then the leg and the delicate toes stretched forward, entering the water with scarcely a ripple, the weight of the body transferred, the other leg following. All in perfectly controlled slow motion. The fishing position unaltered. Eyes on the water, beak forward, ready.

This was Hamlet's bird. You remember where Hamlet, feigning madness, said he knew the difference between a hawk and a handsaw? He didn't mean handsaw but heronshaw, a young heron. The misprint has been handed down unchanged to puzzled generations of theatre-goers ever since. Shakespeare would have seen the herons fishing the banks of the Stratford Avon and, looking up, he would have seen the kestrel hovering above, hunting the meadow. The hunters of river and field.

A flash. So fast you could barely see it. A glint of silver in the bird's mouth. A toss of the head, a swallow, a slight ruff and glissading movement of the bird's neck feathers as the fish went down. That was all. One small trout the less. It was so skilful I felt I should applaud. After all, we were both fishermen.

THE fox bounded across the lane, missing the car by inches, and vanished through a hole in the hedge with a wave from its tail. Not often you see foxes as close as that in daylight, though at night you will and sometimes see jewels of eyes flash fire from your headlights. Fascinating things, foxes.

The best view I ever had of a fox was when it was being chased by hounds across a field with the hunt in full cry behind, just like a Christmas-card scene, galloping horses, pink-coated huntsmen, hounds spread out over the field, the fox well in the lead. Most dramatic and exciting, like charging cavalry. The fox, I was pleased to learn later, got away.

I am not on the side of fox hunting, or to be more accurate I have an ambivalent attitude towards it. I dislike the thought of a wild creature, vermin or otherwise, whatever they may be called, being hounded to death; and a hound's kill is not always so painless or quick as some like to make out. To that extent I am anti-hunt.

On the other hand, and there is always another hand, in sparsely populated country districts, like Devon where I now live, the hunt has a considerable social value. It brings people together, it fills the empty hours after harvest, it gives a scattered community a sense of companionship and a shared interest. There is great enjoyment in a gallop across wild country, a spice of danger, the excitement of the chase, the care of horses and hounds, the fun of the Boxing Day meet outside the local pub, the stirrup cup, the dinners and dances and the great hunt ball.

154

Certainly, there is no doubt, if there were no hunting the country would lose far more than the hunt.

And yet, on the other hand, what would one do about the fox? Those people whose lives are bounded by the towns know little or nothing about the depredation of foxes, but country people do, especially farmers, for they know firsthand the extent of the fox's appetite for ducks and hens and new-born lambs. Foxes are prolific breeders and down here, in Devon, by September the country is full of them, with cubs playing happily outside their dens in the late evening sunshine. How is the farmer to protect his chickens and his lambs? Snares mean a slow and horrible death. Shooting is better, providing of course there is a clean kill, and this is a problem, for how many times are you likely to get a good clean shot? Not all that many times. A wounded fox may linger for days or weeks until hunger or gangrene kills it.

In recent years, something new has happened: the arrival of the hunt saboteurs, small groups of militants who disrupt meets, shout slogans, throw pepper at horses, poison hounds, and daub huntsmen's graves. Their intentions must, in their own eyes, be honourable, in that they hope the publicity will create a public opinion in favour of abolishing hunting. With me it has had an opposite effect. Terrorists of any kind have to be fought. I sent a subscription to my local hunt.

155

Time past time

TROUT is a word that has a pleasant sound. For some reason or other, possibly from its long associations, it conjures up the right kind of image. We see at once the shape of the fish. We see its colour. We see it swaying between weeds, a sudden flicker of the tail. *Flicker, flicker,* and it has gone. A trout. No other word would be quite as good.

I suppose you can capture something of it in music. Schubert did. But in the beginning was the word. It must go back to the Bronze Age and beyond. The Romans had a word like it, taken from the Greeks, so perhaps it came to us with the Roman legions through France, where it stopped off as *truite*, though in Germany it must have come from the roots of another language, *forelle*.

But I like to think of it as an old English word, old when the sarsen stones were sledged along the track to Stonehenge for the summer festivals; old when Maldon was fought, when the first baskets of earth were laid for Avebury. The Beaker folk or

156

someone even earlier who lived in the little villages who helped make Silbury would go down the slope from there to the nearest river, which we now call the Kennet, and take the fish, which they called *truht*, with their nets or baited bone hooks. Some early genius must have given the fish the name and he named it well. An old English word. *Truht*.

No one can be certain of this; only that the word is very old and that is really all that can be said. But to think of the early fishermen when you are fishing the Kennet or the little Lambourn near by, is in some strange way to reach out to the past:

> It is fitting that we should sometimes remember perhaps when the trout are not rising that our Stone Age ancestors stood on the very bank where we now stand, peering like us into the same river and preparing traps for the fish which must have been an important part of their daily food.

Not that you will do so deliberately; but suddenly, out of the blue as it were, the idea may occur to you, as if some early memory has jogged the mind. You will think to yourself that you are standing where others have stood before and you will look up and see the barrows on the chalk downs where some of the early kings or chieftans of this part of the world were buried, and the idea, if it has not already done so, will germinate. You have been here before.

When you come to think of it, the rivers are great survivors of past time, not in the shape nor in the quality that they once had, for they have been trimmed and confined and built over, and boreholes sunk to tap their springs, so that we cannot now imagine what they were like when the wolves and the mammoth came down to the shallows to drink, but it is perhaps not all that important. The river is still there. The ancient trackways, the standing stones, and the barrows are there too.

Even if we are not conscious of them, if the stones and the barrows and the hills are a mere pastoral background which we take for granted, if we have no thought of the past at all, if all our concentration is on the rise of a trout and the presentation of a fly; even so, I think a subtle influence is exerted upon us by our surroundings. What it is I do not know. It could be nothing but a fanciful idea. At the same time we are part of our surroundings and our surroundings are time past.

WALKING the banks of the Kennet, a few hundred yards downstream of the bridge which carries the traffic of the Great West Road, you come to a pool called the Wine Cellar. The river deepens here and big trout lie under the shade of willows. The branches hang down low over the water and the occasional shred of nylon hanging from them marks the place where fishermen have been at work. They have been at work in the Wine Cellar pool of the Kennet for more than six hundred years, for this is the town fishery which was given to Hungerford by John O'Gaunt at some time in the mid 1300s and has had a continuous recorded history ever since.

John O'Gaunt – described by Shakespeare in *Richard II*, you may remember, as 'time-honoured Lancaster' – was one of the battling dukes of the Wars of the Roses. He acquired his Hungerford estates by marriage to Blanche of Hungerford and gave the fishery to the Commoners of the town for sheltering his army during one of his campaigns. The gift infuriated his descendants, who tried by every means to get it back, and it was not until a couple of hundred years later, during the reign of Elizabeth, that the Queen confirmed to the town of Hungerford 'such liberties and profits and benefits as heretofore, time out of mind and the remembrance of man, they have used and enjoyed.'

Those who know today's Statutory Orders may well envy the Elizabethans their language. The words are precise and accurate in their elegance, and can, with only a minor stretch of the imagination, suggest that all that now remains in the remembrance of man is the name of the pool where Blanche of Hungerford used to cool her wine.

Whatever the origin of the name of the Wine Cellar pool – and there is no reason why it should not go back to medieval times – it is the deepest pool nearest to the town and most likely to have been the one netted to provide 'the good troute' which Samuel Pepys had for dinner, when he stayed at the Bear Inn. Odds and scraps of time past come crowding upon you when you sit by the pool and wait for the rise, thoughts of men who have fished here before, casting a fly up under the willow on the right bank, or across to the willow from the opposite bank, a delicate business, however skilful a man may be with rod and line.

Perhaps the impression of time past is still there in some unaccountable way, for even without knowing the history of the place you are aware, as you approach, that the pool has an atmosphere. Perhaps the shades of many anglers are there. Perhaps when we see the rings of a rising fish intangible hands are with ours as we lift the rod. It is not too much of a conceit. The hands are those we have inherited and are those within our own.

BEHIND the cottage on the other side of the lane is a cliff. many millions of years ago it must have been a wave of liquid magma, pushed out from the great volcanic eruptions that made Dartmoor but now it is a tranquil place of scrub oak and hazel, alder and rhododendrons, all so overgrown that even small boys from the village find it impenetrable. That is fortunate, as rumour has it that somewhere in the steep tangle of bushes there is an open mine shaft where prospectors looked for tin or copper, arsenic, or gold. But these are rumours.

The cliff is not all that high, maybe a hundred or two hundred feet, but because it is so difficult for men to climb it has become a sanctuary for wild things. Buzzards breed there and badgers have found enough earth amid the rocks to make their setts.

Once, when we were driving up the lane to go sea-trout fishing at night, a badger was trotting along ahead of us. A badger waggles its backside when it trots, like a grey mat being shaken. Brock looked round once into the glare of the headlights but did not go any faster and we had to slow down not to run too close. 'Badger,' we cried. 'Badger!' He took no notice. After a while he turned off into the bushes and we had the impression he had gone where he wanted and had not been disturbed by the car and the lights. A fox would have been too scared to behave like that.

Sometimes a badger will cross the lane and come through a hole in the hedgerow into our garden. We don't see much of them. They come at night, sometimes in the morning we may see some droppings or a little scrape where they've scratched a hole in the lawn. Perhaps they look for moles. Perhaps they like to mark their territorial boundaries. Perhaps they like to dig. Maybe they come into the garden to reach our pond or the river to have a drink. The river is at the bottom of our garden under a screen of trees. Small brown trout live in it and from mid-summer onwards there are shoals of sea trout in the deeper pools and an occasional salmon.

When I first came to live here I would fish the pool just above the bridge, a shallow pool with a fast run by the bushes on the far bank. The river is a spate river rising and falling with every drop of rain from the moors, and even here in the valley it is rocky and rugged and has many variations of current and flow. There is little weed in the water, for if ever it does establish itself the winter floods sweep it away. Consequently the trout are hungry and never grow big.

There were many of them at one time, and once, in the pool above the bridge, I took nine fish one after the other, fishing the edge of the fast water by the far bank with a pattern of a spent dun, allowing it to sink a little. The fish came to it fast, like lightning, and you had to tighten without waiting as soon as you saw the rise. They were all small, the largest no more than eight or ten ounces, but they were a bright buttercup yellow with scarlet and carmine spots, typical wild moorland-born trout.

160

There are not so many in the river now. There is too much pollution from the farms.

I WAS, for some years, fortunate enough to live in an apartment block that overlooked the Thames at Teddington. There was a marina just below our windows which was full of little boats that never seemed to do anything but stay there, though once or twice some of the bigger ones had parties on board and pretty girls sun-bathing on the roof. But the main interest was that the marina was the home of a family of Canada geese. They were wise birds. Whenever they came to harbour all the apartment windows in the nine-storey block would open and showers of bread would go down on to the water and the surrounding grass like manna from heaven. The geese prospered.

Occasionally, in the evening, when there were not many people in the swimming-pool, which was next to the river, I would go down to the river's edge and practise casting. I never caught much, a gudgeon or two and a small roach, that was about all, for that part of the Thames held no trout.

But there are trout in the Thames, mainly in the big weir pools, at the edges of the flow, at places like Staines and Chertsey, but they are unlikely to be taken on a fly, except perhaps a salmon fly, for they are great predators and live on the shoals of bleak and gudgeon.

I doubt if they are much fished for now but they were at one time, in Victorian and Edwardian days. The great masters of Thames trout fishing, mainly on a spun bleak, were Patrick Chalmers and A. E. Hobbs. Indeed Hobbs fished the Thames for 55 years, up to and including 1945. During that time he caught 878 trout over three pounds, all wild browns and quite a number below that weight, which he returned to the water. He saw at least six trout which he put in the 15 to 20 lb class. The largest, of 17 lb 3 oz, was on the slab in a fishmonger's shop in Maidenhead and had been taken by a poacher on a nightline.

161

Hobbs' biggest trout was just short of 10 lb but he lost a much bigger one at Marsh Weir. He was fishing a dead bleak mounted on a trace and was winding it in on the edge of quiet water when a fish took and plunged powerfully into the depths. After about a quarter of an hour he managed to bring it to the surface, where he saw it long enough to convince himself that this was the fish of a lifetime, well into double figures. Then came tragedy. The lock-keeper tried to net the fish out too early, one of the hooks caught in the net, and the fish tore itself free.

IT is sometimes thought that chalk-stream fishing is a rigid discipline. One must always match the fly on the water. It is not so. It is nothing of the kind:

> A good fish was lying near the surface. He looked at but refused a Tup. I tried several other flies and to each, when he saw them for the first time, he gave a critical but dispassionate inspection, but after that he took no more notice than he would of a pound note. The light breeze had been killed by the sun, the air was glowing, and the surface of the water like burnished steel. Almost in despair I tied on a Caperer. It fell with a flop and looked like a dead cockchafer but the trout had it at once.

The man who wrote that passage was a great dry-fly purist, a follower of Halford and one who knew him well – John Waller Hills, who wrote one of the most delightful books imaginable, *A Summer on the Test*. Hills, like Edward Grey, was a fishing politican, a Government minister who escaped down to the Test at Stockbridge whenever he could get away. He was a tolerant man in an age of intolerance.

It must be nearly fifty years since Hills died but his writing is as fresh and vivid as ever. He was an admirer of Skues and thought that nymph fishing was possibly more skilful than fishing the dry fly. When he was uncertain what fly to use for the Test he would pick out a North Country wet fly, the Orange Partridge, which he fished in the surface film. I have followed his advice on many occasions and believe that the fly must suggest a half-drowned spinner.

If you haven't read Hills you may be nervous about the choice of fly for a chalk stream. I know I was. When I was first taken to – I think it was the Itchen – I was nervous about using any pattern but the orthodox split-wing floater, and would never cast to a trout unless it was on the fin and rising to the surface to take the occasional fly. This, I was assured, was the right thing to do, and so I did it. I kept all my wet flies rigidly separate in separate boxes and left them in the car. Yet a really good wet fly can sometimes do as much damage, or even more, than the dry. Read Skues.

Not that I don't like the dry fly, of course I do, but the point is that one should not be rigid about it, one should always experiment, do this, do that, do the other, sink your spinner if they won't take it floating, cast across and down with your dry fly if you can't cast up.

Even Halford wasn't as rigid in his later years as he was at the beginning. He was certainly less rigid than some of his followers. He even admitted there were times when it was best to cast a dry fly downstream. He also suggested fishing the water:

> There are some purists who will only cast to rising fish but that is in my opinion riding the hobby to death, and I for one am a strong advocate for floating a cocked fly over a likely place, even if not a movement of a feeding fish has been seen there.

Matching the hatch may well be necessary on some occasions but by no means all. Some of our great chalk-stream fishermen will tell you that presentation is far more important. Whether this is so, because most of our chalk streams are now full of hatchery trout I am not certain. Frank Sawyer was among those

163

who thought that hatchery trout were much less discriminating in their choice of fly than wild fish. It could be so. In any case it is an additional argument in favour of an independent outlook on our choice of fly, a further support for the idea of the liberal-minded purist.

Have you seen my husband?

~~~⊃◦◎◦⊂~~~

MEMBERS do not wish to be addressed whilst covering a fish, says the guide to members' behaviour in the rules of one of our oldest fishing clubs. How right they are. I should hate to be addressed whilst covering a fish. There are not all that many fish that you can cover these days and when you find a good one and are looking for something to cover it with – an Iron Blue perhaps or possibly a Black Gnat – it would be quite the wrong time for someone to start to address us. Fishermen are, on the whole, among the mildest of men but there is nothing so calculated to arouse their worst instincts as when some genial character asks, no doubt in the politest and most interested way, whether we've had any luck.

One immediately has to stifle back some discourteous monosyllable to the effect that we haven't. On the other hand, if we say that we have, it leads almost inevitably to further enquiries and to what may well become a prolonged and tedious conversation. One might even be asked or expected to show one's catch. All in all, it is difficult to know quite how to respond, especially if the man is a fellow member of the club and is anxious to show goodwill. One could of course begin with a long dissertation on the place of luck in fly fishing and whether that is of more importance than skill and observation, but the danger is not only the amount of time it would take up, but the further disadvantage that it might well put us down among the club bores.

Members are by no means the only culprits, for the wives of members who occasionally arrive on the fishery to remind their errant husbands that they are long overdue for some crucial appointment or other have a habit of addressing everyone in earshot, irrespective of whether they are covering or uncovering a fish, a distinction which they would probably find incomprehensible anyway.

Teetering along the bank in their high shoes from the car park – they have just come from shopping or something and have no boots – they call to the nearest man for help, and he, poor chap, feels impelled to come to her aid even though her erring husband may be two stiles and three fields away upstream. But that is not all. Worse than that can happen. Much worse. It happened to me and I still feel embarrassed at the memory.

I was after a fish. I had been covering it for something like an hour, but it felt longer. It was a particularly difficult fish, by a weed bed. I had tried everything and once or twice the fish had looked and gone away. Tension had grown and grown until, in various ways, mental and physical, I was almost at bursting point. I was quite unaware of my surroundings. All my concentration was on the fish.

Unexpectedly it rose and I struck too soon. I felt the fish for a brief moment but that was all. The tension in me exploded. I let out a great blast of wind and an obscene curse. Exactly at the moment those sounds filled the air came a girl's voice:

'Excuse me, have you seen my husband?'

She was a very pretty girl in a flowery summer dress, standing close by my side, who had crept up on me from the car park. I gasped. I stuttered. I went very red. It ruined the rest of my day!

CURIOUS things do happen from time to time. There was, for example, the case of the alligator in the Itchen.

A dry fly man who had a beautiful stretch of the river below Winchester was peacefully walking the banks looking for a rise when he saw something odd halfway across near the far bank. The thing, whatever it was, behaved as though it was alive and he could not be certain of this, but he thought he could see an eye. He didn't like the look of it.

He knew there was a man fishing the next beat so he turned and traipsed back along the bank, very puzzled and irritated. He found the man concentrating on a fish, so he had to wait for a bit, hopping up and down impatiently, and eventually the chap got fed up and asked what he wanted. It wasn't exactly a warm welcome.

Anyway, the man said he'd like the chap to come and look at something, and the chap said, 'What?' He said he didn't know but it was something odd. So they walked back to where the thing had been, and there it was, still in the same place. They looked at it, and the thing opened an eye and looked back at them. Then it gave a demonstration of swimming, going round in a circle and then into the reeds. From there it looked at them again. Coyly it seemed, as if it was having a kind of game.

'What do you make of it?' said the man.

167

'Most extraordinary,' said the chap from the other beat. 'Have you seen any of them before?'

The alligator had another swim round and they watched it for some time. The man who had seen it first thought it was a large lizard of some kind, but the chap who'd come up from the other beat was pretty certain it was not a lizard, or a young crocodile, but an alligator because it had a rather short broad head and crocodiles hadn't. As he'd been in America and had a nodding acquaintance with alligators they decided that's what it was. They spent some time deciding what to do but the alligator decided for them by plunging down and coming up with a trout in its mouth. Trout were scarce enough as it was without alligators.

They went along to the nearest 'phone box, a couple of miles away, and put through a nine-nine-nine call to the police. When they said they'd found an alligator in the Itchen the police told them to pull the other one, but they swore it was true and as there were two of them seeing things the police thought they might as well believe them. So the two of them went back and waited by the gate in the field for half-an-hour or so and eventually the police arrived. Behind them was a fire engine and an ambulance.

By now there was quite a crowd by the river and the alligator had become shy and hidden itself in the reeds, but the chap who knew alligators probed about with a stick and the alligator didn't like that and came out in full view. It may sound odd but nobody had thought to bring a net with them. One of the police wanted to shoot it but this was thought unwise in case it was a valuable alligator and they would have to pay compensaton. Eventually another policeman went off to find a river warden or someone who might have a net and after about half-an-hour came back with a rather thin mesh net he'd borrowed from a fruit-farmer. There was now the problem how to get it over the alligator, which had gone to a weed bed in the middle of the stream. The afternoon was getting rather cold and dark and the firemen thought it was about time they were going home. The ambulance men said they would stay on, in case.

The ambulance men were very chatty and said they'd never

treated alligator bites before so it was something to write about to the St John's and the Red Cross if they did, and they were looking up their books and deciding the best thing to do would be to treat it as a dog bite and get the anti-tetanus in quick. They had a long chat with the chap from the other beat who was knowledgeable about alligators, and was looked upon as something of an expert, and he told them how the kids in New York, who were given baby alligators as presents, had to get rid of them when they grew big so they swilled them down the lavatories and the sewers of New York became full of alligators, and those that survived the treatment got out into the Madison River and swam south, home to the Everglades. It was a nice story and after seeing an alligator in the Itchen they could believe anything.

Two of the policemen, having borrowed waders from the fishermen, were now trying to throw the net over the alligator without much success, for the net floated and when it did fall over the alligator's head, as it did once, the creature sank and swam off to a deeper part of the river. There was a good deal of shouting and argument and everyone giving advice, most of it useless, and the police were more or less up to their chests in the water now, and shivering. They'd tried everything. The trout landing-nets were too small, the fruit net had torn and they couldn't make it sink. They were about to give up when a local fish-farmer turned up with a big hand-made net which he used for stocking the river. After half-an-hour or so chasing the alligator from one part of the river to the next, the fish-farmer finally got him in his big net. The police wrapped the remains of the fruit net round both the big net and the alligator, and carried off their prize in triumph to be put into a bath in a house near the police station, while they 'made enquiries'. Eventually they were able to return the poor creature to its rightful owner. It had escaped from a private zoo.

The fishermen were very fed up with the whole thing. The alligator hunt had put down every trout for miles and there was no possibility of an evening rise.

A Fly on the Water

I HAVE a strange reluctance about meeting mink. It is not really surprising. Most people have a reluctance about meeting somebody or something. One of our Foreign Secretaries was so reluctant about meeting an American President that whenever there was a danger of it he would have a cold, or a headache, or go fishing. That is the kind of relationship I have with mink.

Curiously enough I do not feel the same about meeting otters or stoats and weasels, only mink. I think it must be the way they look at you. They don't seem afraid of you, as they should. Once, when I was sitting on the river bank eating my sandwiches, a mink ran over my legs, taking a short cut somewhere. I don't like that kind of behaviour. An otter wouldn't have done it.

Mink have the same arrogance when they go hunting. I was once wading the River Lyd near my home, casting upstream to a few rising trout in Clare Pool and I had reached the place where there is a nasty steep shelf of rock and the water deepens, so that you have to be careful not to get the water over the top of your waders. Just as I was getting into a little local difficulty there I was passed by a mink swimming very fast upstream, not more than a foot or so away from me. An otter would have had more decency than to swim past me like that without so much as a by-your-leave, but this mink didn't care. He turned off sharply under some bushes on the near bank and after a great scuffle and screaming he came out with a rabbit, a big one. They kept turning over and over in the water, struggling and shouting and splashing. I prodded them with my landing net to see if I could knock them apart, but it had no effect and they went splashing off downstream and I went into the water, over the top of my waders. The next thing I saw was the rabbit running up the bank, into the field, with the mink hanging on to its throat. After that came a terrible screaming from the rabbit which got fainter and fainter but seemed to last a long time before it was silenced. Otters wouldn't have done that. Not in public.

The only other creature of that size about which I am apprehensive is the ferret. I looked up ferret in the dictionary the other day and was surprised to find it described as a half-tamed albino variety of the polecat. Half-tamed, I would agree, even though some countrymen carry them inside their shirt, but why an albino polecat should be more amenable to training than an ordinary polecat I have no idea. Possibly an albino polecat suffers some kind of feral inferiority which makes it more amenable to man.

Mink are not amenable. An Irish angler, spinning the Barrow for sea trout, hooked a mink which played him for a while, then climbed out on the bank and ran away across the field. The angler was lucky. Most mink would have hit back.

Hero figures

IT was once said of one of our former Prime Ministers, Harold Macmillan, that when he was hailed in the newspapers as Supermac he felt a considerable temptation to believe it. The same is probably true of the angler who was described some

172

years ago in one of our more exuberant magazines as Britain's Number One Nymph Fisherman.

Sporting journals have the same inclination to mythology as do the newspapers, for the idealised hero-figure is as old as Odysseus, probably much older, and contains more than a grain of truth, even if, as invariably happens, it is overlaid by invention.

The change from being one of the crowd, an ordinary angler, to being a leading figure among trout fishermen may well be taken at first as being a due recognition of achievement. But there are subtle and significant disadvantages.

The Number One Nymph Fisherman will have to accustom himself to the fact that unless he decamps to an uninhabited island, or one of the remotest of hill lochs, he will never again be able to go fishing in peace, never able to buy a day ticket and wade out among his fellows in decent obscurity. He will be a marked man. Every move he makes will be under scrutiny; the strength of his casting, the distance achieved, the rate of retrieve, the length and strength of his leader, the make of his rods, the colour of his lines, all will be analysed, recorded and discussed.

He will be pursued by rod makers who will want him to sign contracts that will give his name to their products, by club secretaries who want him to address their annual meetings (as often as not without fee), and by admirers who would like to ghost a book for him. Photographers will dog his footsteps, writers will arrive with notebooks and tape recorders, fishery-managers provide free passes for him in the hope that he will catch their specially stocked and specially fattened record rainbows before a gallery of excited fans.

The trouble comes, of course, when he begins to believe in the myth that has been created about him, when the illusion persists that he really is the infallible fisherman, the legendary nymph man who will take fish after fish in a dead calm during a heat-wave and have his limit before anyone else has caught anything at all. It may well have happened once but when it seems unlikely to happen again, or even again, he will begin to worry, and at that stage he may also wonder why his fishing is not quite so enjoyable as it was.

His family will be the first to notice the transformation, the long silences, the brooding glances, the abstracted air, the intentness with which he sets out in the morning and the despair with which he returns well after dark. There is little they can do to restore his spirit, to help him regain balance, to forget his public image, his title and his admirers. A myth is dangerous.

BING CROSBY'S pipe is now in a museum in Manchester, Vermont. So are the rods and flies that were once used by Eisenhower, Herbert Hoover, Carnegie and Ernest Hemingway. How many rods and flies and fishing bags that once belonged to the famous are now stored in the beautiful and elegant series of rooms of the American Museum of Fly Fishing is difficult to say, but quite a number. They have added Crosby's well-chewed briar pipe, seen not only on films but in fishing lodges in Alaska and Iceland, to his cherished collection of rods and flies.

There is much to be said for collections. They must be open to the general public even if a large majority of the general public is disinterested. The interest of the few will make up for much. Sponsorship is almost inevitable, and in America that has been generously supplied, so that the museum not only has a fine building but tours exhibitions and publishes a magazine.

In this country most of our fishing memorabilia is in private hands. Halford and Skues' flies and rods are in the possession of the Flyfishers' Club, which also has a Walton creel in a showcase which may or may not have belonged to Izaak but which is certainly authentic seventeenth century. There are some other notable private collections which are occasionally on show to the public, but that is about all. Much is missing, including the rods and tackle used by such men as Plunket Greene and Edward Grey, though there is a fine portrait of Grey in the dining room of the United Oxford and Cambridge Universities' Club.

174

British Prime Ministers seem to have been more inclined to shoot grouse than go fishing, though Lord Home, then Sir Alec Douglas Home, did manage a cast or two on the Tweed while he was in Downing Street, and Neville Chamberlain wielded a rod from time to time, though on balance American fly-fishing Presidents outnumber our fly-fishing Prime Ministers by about five to two.

Lord Home has written evocatively about fishing, but pride of place here may well remain with Edward Grey, who was our Foreign Secretary for about 15 years before and during World War I. He it was who made the famous remark, on the outbreak of the war, about the lights of Europe going out one by one. Grey's hobby was looked upon with some curiosity at the time, certainly by the Prime Minister, Lloyd George, who is on record as saying, 'Grey would have risen to great heights if he hadn't wasted his time fishing.' Time has had its turn. Lloyd George's memoirs are long out of print. Edward Grey's *Fly Fishing* has just been republished.

READERS of Hornblower may remember the time when he was captured by the French, escaped, and took refuge in the house of a French nobleman, the Compte de Gracay, in his home on the banks of the Loire. With Hornblower were his servant, Brown, and Lieutenant Bush. They laid plans for a return to England by boating down the Loire and capturing a sea-going vessel at Nantes. They needed to be disguised, as Napoleon's police would be on the lookout, so they chose to be fishermen.

Three men in a rowing boat would be able to avoid staying at inns or seeking the shelter of houses. They would sleep on the bank, avoiding all intercourse with Frenchmen, and would drift downstream until they reached the sea.

'If you have fishing rods with you,' the Compte de Gracay told Hornblower, 'anyone observing you go past the towns will look on you as a fishing party out for the day. For some reason which I cannot fully analyse, a freshwater fisherman can never be suspected of evil intent − except possibly by the fish.'

There is a good deal to be said for that point of view. Certainly, for Hornblower and his party, the scheme worked well enough all the way to Nantes where, after further adventures, they captured a brig and returned to England in triumph. It helped, of course, that in those days there were no river wardens, no *gardiens*, in their green uniforms, to ask to see the licences and permits. All the same, it is true to say that even today, with a very different climate of opinion, the average man drifting down a river with his fishing rod is almost certainly a law-abiding character whose name is not normally on the case lists at the Old Bailey.

He may, of course, be guilty of a petty offence, such as worming, or using mayfly nymphs during a hatch of fly, but that will probably be as far as depravity goes. Bank robbers might have thought of drifting down the Thames as far as Wapping Old Stairs to board fast cruisers that would take them to safety in some far-distant Latin American republic, but if so there has been no mention of it in the newspapers or on the radio. One can assume that fishermen do not normally think of becoming bank robbers, partly no doubt because the planning and execution of a raid would take up so much fishing time which could be more usefully spent in other ways. No one whose main interest in life is whether an Orange Quill is a substitute for the Blue-winged Olive can be a satisfactory member of a gang absorbed in the study of sewers beneath the exposed vaults of Williams and Glyns. Like the roach fisherman who was found wandering in the City in the early hours of the morning and was taken before the magistrate for loitering with intent, he has only to declare himself as a fisherman on his way to the river to be discharged without a stain on his character.

One suspects that the Compte de Gracay was right, and that from the point of view of the police as well as of the criminal classes, your average fisherman must be regarded as a very dubious catch.

TO say that a man has gone fishing carries less social stigma than most other excuses for his being absent from work. He is not likely to be thought neglecting his business quite so much as if he were playing golf, an indulgence sometimes excused as an opportunity for making contacts, generally undefined, or the entertaining of important customers. Going sailing or shooting are on the whole weekend activities and not generally accepted as a good reason for being away in working hours, while to say that a man has gone mountaineering is as good as admitting he need not be expected back in his office until next week at the earliest.

Perhaps the tolerance allowed to a man who goes fishing is partly because we have been processed into believing that it is a contemplative man's recreation, which cannot be said of other outdoor activities, and therefore virtuous, though in a way not easily defined. A man may contemplate a float for hours without necessarily being improved as a result. In fact it is quite likely that for most of the time he may not be taking part in any self-improvement at all. His mind may have lapsed into a complete blank. This may be a good therapy but can hardly be said to be contemplation.

Fly fishing is certainly not a sport for men who have a leaning to the contemplative life. A salmon fisherman, let us say, who is covering difficult lies in fast water has not much time to concentrate on anything as abstract as the immutability of human affairs, nor for that matter a reservoir fisherman closely engaged in a double haul. There are times, it is true, when a chalk-stream fisherman may sit for some hours waiting for a hatch, but instead of brooding on absolutes and the cloud of unknowing, he is almost certainly suffering from boredom and dark thoughts.

True, there are exceptions, such as the case, not long ago, when a City businessman was reputed to have worked out all the permutations for a takeover bid for one of our larger industrial undertakings while fishing the dry fly on a major chalk-stream. But although the bid was ultimately successful, his fishing, according to at least one eye-witness, was not. To concentrate on the job in hand, one must assume, is advice that applies to fly fishing as much as anything else.

The true addict, the natural born fishermen, is by no means content to practise in his spare time what is misleadingly described as a hobby. He will make time, even if he has to go to some lengths to do so. One high court judge was absent from the bench for so many notably long periods that he was said to have taken up fly fishing as his profession, returning to the courts only when he needed the money to continue. There was the case of the London solicitor who recruited as many clients as possible in the area of the Itchen valley so as to enable him to study the life cycle of the Baetis nymph, a work for which, incidentally, he became famous. Then there was the surgeon who gave up a lucrative practice in Harley Street for a poor one in an obscure Wiltshire village so that, after an hour or so with patients in the morning he could put up a notice '*Gone Fishing*' in the surgery window and depart. From all this evidence – and these are but a few of the authenticated cases – there is not much doubt that a man sufficiently determined to do so will find a way of practising his vocation in spite of his work.

Literary fishes

=◦◊◦=

I DOUBT very much if any other period of history has seen such an outburst of creative writing about fishing as occurred during the ten or fifteen years or so before and after the 1914–1918 war. Halford had thrown a bombshell into trout fishing on the chalk-streams; Skues was fighting hard to reverse the dominance of the ultra-purists, and Grey, Plunket Greene and Waller Hills were writing of the pleasures of fishing in a way that had never been attempted before, or which, if it had been attempted, had never matured into such a civilised and urbane style as they managed to achieve. Above all else was Arthur Ransome's fishing column in the *Manchester Guardian* which used what so many had thought was a mundane sport as a touchstone of life and art. Ransome, already a delightful teller of children's tales, used his essays on fishing to illuminate a philosophy. Curiously enough, at more or less the same time, a writer on cricket in the same paper, Neville Cardus, was doing the same thing. It is worth quoting what Cardus said:

To go to a cricket match for nothing but cricket is as though a man were to go into an inn for nothing but drink. As I look back on my twenty years in the sun (sometimes it rained) I can scarcely believe that all the juicy characters I came to know on cricket fields have actually existed. I get them confused with the creations of the nation's comic writers. Emmot Robinson of Yorkshire; Rhodes and Hirst; Maurice Leyland and Parkin – they all come back to my mind endowed with the gusto of human genius; they are as satisfying to my sense of comedy as anybody in the range of comic literature.

Ransome, of course – well, indeed, you can quote Ransome on almost anything – comedy or otherwise – and it will be illuminating. Take the opening sentence of one of his many perfect essays, that on *Tackle* Shops:

The pleasures of fishing are chiefly to be found in rivers, lakes and tackle-shops, and of the three, the last are least affected by the weather.

One reads Ransome with a growing, an exhilarating, pleasure. We have written about him already, and quoted him too, so we must restrain our enthusiasm, otherwise his publisher or his estate will be claiming royalties, but his *Advice to Beginners* is so superb that I am forced to take that risk. Here is what he says:

Fortunately, in fishing we are beginners all. Fishing is not like billiards, in which it is possible to obtain a disgusting perfection. It is not like chess, in which a sharp line seems to be drawn between those who play badly enough to enjoy the game and those who play so well that they have lost all spirit of adventure and haggle over pawns like misers over pence. The older a fisherman grows the more conscious is he that he has much to learn and he lays aside his rod in the end as a man dies, knowing that all his effort has left him but a bungler. The better a fisherman is, the more conscious is he of his imperfections and consequently the more shy of giving advice to others. He is also likely to have learnt that the chief pleasure of fishing is to be still beginning and, unselfishly, he will be very unwilling to steal from a beginner any of the delights of finding out for himself.

So it goes on, each sentence, each phrase and the timing of the phrase, polished like diamonds. He may have written that passage half a dozen times, maybe a dozen, before he came to that finely engineered precision of the prose; the placing of the word *all* after *beginners* instead of before it, to give the sentence an appropriate fall; to find the right adjective to describe the perfection of the professional billiards player − in our day no doubt he would have written snooker instead of billiards. No matter. Only a few will be aware of the laborious mining and shaping of words and sentences behind an apparently easy perfection. It is the same with most of the arts and crafts, whether the timing and phrasing of an actor, the shaping of a pot by the potter, the intricate construction of a symphony. All need work as well as genius; indeed much of a part of genius arrives from work. Certainly, it was so with Ransome.

It would be wrong to imagine, however, that because a man was a great essayist he had no concern for the practical side of fishing, not only wrong but foolish, yet the mistake is not unlikely in our own time, which has seen the publication of so many practical textbooks, and authoritative guides on not only how to fish, but how to succeed in fishing, and one I remember that sought to reduce fishing to a science. Ransome is full of practical advice, so are Waller Hills and Greene, but with it they widen our horizons. Edward Grey chose our salmon flies but gave us also this unforgettable description of a man on his way to use them:

Often after walking a mile or two on the way to the river, at a brisk pace, there comes upon one a feeling of 'fitness', of being made of nothing but health and strength so perfect, that life need have no other end but to enjoy them. It is as though till that moment one had breathed with only a part of one's lungs, and as though now for the first time the whole lungs were filling with air. The pure act of breathing at such times seems glorious. People talk of being a child of nature, and moments such as these are the times when it is possible to feel so; to know the full joy of animal life – to desire nothing beyond. There are times when I have stood still for joy of it all, on my way through the wild freedom of a Highland moor, and felt the wind, and looked upon the mountains and water and light and sky, till I felt conscious only of a mighty current of life, which swept away all consciousness of self, and made me a part of all I beheld.

We are back here, to use the word in the widest possible sense, to the feel of a religious experience, which was paramount in Walton, Berners, and many earlier writers, though in Grey moving closer in the direction of pantheism than the early canonicals would have approved.

Not that all the experiences of fishermen focus upon, or are directly derived from, either conventional or even unconventional religious emotions, if that is how Grey's apparent pantheism may be described. There is no need to invent a religious excuse for the pleasure of hunting. It is sufficient that we are with rod-and-line in the wilderness and enjoying ourselves. Grey, however, was a forerunner for essayists still to be born, notably in our own time the American writer, Nick Lyons.

The English fisherman must allow for the American idiom to appreciate Lyons to the full, or perhaps one might even say the American language, for there are growing distinctions, but Lyons stands up to it pretty well, perhaps because he is also, in another manifestation, an associate professor of English in one of America's universities. Like it or not, the English fisherman owes a great deal now to the Americans, including most of our rods and tackle; and in the last forty or fifty years some of the finest writing about fly fishing has come from the other side of the Atlantic. Lyons is closer to us than some of his fellow-Americans. His writing follows more the classical tradition that we find familiar, absorbing it, making use of it, yet with a sudden twist of meaning and use of words that can only come to a man who lives and works in New York. If there is pantheism here, it is absorbed, if not liquidated, by other experiences and explanations. When he manages to get away from New York to the Catskills or Montana he analyses the reactions in himself in a way that no English writer, or perhaps only a very few, have yet attempted. Like this:

Fishing mkes rivers my corrective lens. I see differently. Not only does the bird taking the mayfly signify a hatch, not only does the flash of color at the break of the riffle signify a fish feeding, but my powers uncoil inside me and I must determine which insect is hatching and what feeding pattern the trout has established. Then I must properly equip myself and properly approach the fish and properly present my imitation. I am engaged in a hunt which is more than a hunt, for the objects of the hunt are mostly to be found within myself, in the nature of my response and action. I am on a Parsifalian quest. I must be scientist, technician, athlete, perhaps even a queer sort of poet.

We must leave it there. It is, and I have just realised it as I write, no bad quotation on which to end.

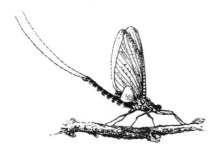

Notes and explanations

I am most grateful to those who have given me permission to quote from their works, and to the holders of copyright, and if any have been inadvertently left out I must apologise for such an oversight. I would also like to be more precise about the location of some of the rivers and lakes mentioned in the text, and to explain the background to some of the stories.

The first chapter, 'The Passionate Fisherman', starts with an essay that is pure fiction for most of the time and more or less wrote itself after I had put down, quite arbitrarily, the opening sentence, which occurred to me in my bath. A bath is a good place for contemplation. The original, in *The Times*, was much shorter and did not have a happy ending, which I think it should have. The Orwell quotation you will find in *The Magic Wheel*, edited by David Profumo and Graham Swift, an invaluable source book (Heineman, 1981). Dr H. B. McCaskie was the brother of Dr Norman McCaskie, creator of McCaskie's Green Cat, and the quotation was from H. B. McCaskie's *The Guileless Trout* (Cresset Press, 1950).

'Fishing is not a game' is a delightful quotation I took from an article

184

in *The Field* which cried out to be made fun of, but I tactfully withhold the name of the author as he might not like being made fun of. The quotation about tribal laws is from *The Management of Angling Waters* (Deutsch, 1977) by Alex Behrendt, doyen of all fishery managers. The man who wrote about trout being star performers, Arnold Gingrich, was the publisher of *Esquire* magazine and author of *The Fishing in Print* (Winchester Press, New York, 1974).

Lionel Sweet was a former world fly-casting champion, who seemed to those who watched him to be able to cast a quarter-of-a-mile, but it might have been less. Jean Williams carries on Sweet's Tackle Shop in Usk, and for anyone near there, staying at The Three Salmons, a visit is imperative. The quotation about fly-casting techniques, 'high, flick, block', is somehow not quite right but is as near as possible to what Charles Ritz used to tell me, accompanied by vivid, though incomprehensible, gestures of the casting arm.

Curiously enough, though no misogynist, I have always been a little suspicious about Dame Juliana Berners. For the explanation I must refer you to Jack Heddon in *The Encyclopedia of Fly Fishing* (Batsford, 1986). Robert Venables you can discover in *The Experienced Angler* (The Antrobus Press, 1969) and one of the best introductions to Skues is in Donald Overfield's *Famous Flies and Their Originators* (Black, 1972).

If you have not read Arthur Ransome's book, *Rod and Line* (Oxford paperback, 1980) you must try to buy it at once; also pester Granada television to show the film of his life, first broadcast on Channel 4 in 1982. I have not yet seen any other television programme on fishing to hold a candle to it.

Dunne you will find in *Sunshine and The Dry Fly* (first edition 1924, second edition Black, 1950), but he is an infuriating man to read as all his flies are tied according to mathematical formulae from materials that are no longer available. For Ted Hughes you should read *Selected Poems, 1967–1981*, and *River*, with photographs by Peter Keen, both published by Faber.

'A Haggis and a Whisky Grog' has been quoted all over the world. I first dicovered it in the library of Laggan House on the Spey in a book by Sir George Aston (*Mostly About Trout*, Allen & Unwin, 1921). The article about Miss Greer was inspired, if inspired is the right word, by a book review by Fay Weldon which I have partially quoted, I hope correctly, to illuminate the destiny of liberated woman. I don't know where the C. B. Fry quotation came from, it may have been in an interview I did with him, or it may have been in one of his books or articles. Sorry.

I was better prepared about Dr Philip Neighbour for I had most of this information from Renée Wilson and the staff of the Salisbury Museum. The last man in England to have been bitten by Dr Johnson's parrot is a very old friend of mine. The incident occurred in The Cheshire Cheese pub, off Fleet Street, in or about 1939. The quotation in the parrot story comes from Edward Grey's *Fly Fishing* (my edition is Dent, 1920, but there have been others, before and since).

'Angels On A Pin' comes from a theological work I once read, but have now forgotten, and is an example of how, with the best will in the world, one can concentrate on the impossible and the absurd. Humpty Dumpty, as you must have known, is from *Alice Through The Looking Glass*. The other quotations in this chapter are: Halford, *Dry Fly Fishing*, 1889; *Fishing Gazette*, no date; Fishing Regulations, Piscatorial Society, c. 1960; *National Angling Survey* and *Angling in Britain*, both 1980; Virginia Woolf is reviewed in *The Magic Wheel*, (Heineman, 1986).

'A Myth Of Flies' mocks the habits of some publishers' copywriters; the eminent scholar is, or was, a member of the RSPCA but his name unfortunately escapes me. I do know who told me about the NATO flies but as he is still subject to army discipline, and as he may have committed an offence under the Official Secrets Act or Queen's Regulations in mentioning the fact that NATO issues flies, his name is withheld. In the story about the dry fly, the old friend of mine was David Jacques and the quotation, again, from Dunne.

'The Taking Place' is about salmon fishing, and the fishing records from *The Encyclopedia of Fly Fishing*. The secret of painless hook removal was shown to me by Roy Buckingham, fishery manager of The Arundel Arms at Lifton, Devon, and the incident of the treble in the bathroom carpet was at the Altnaharra Hotel in Sutherland, both splendid fishing hotels. The advertisement for the fishing lodge to which you have to bring your own cook came from Strutt and Parker, who think of everything.

'Blue Charm' had to be written, and is a true story, about the Lower Floors beat of the Tweed, but the story about the six fishermen who never came back is fishing-hut gossip and though it may be true, I cannot vouch for it. Scrope's *Days And Nights Of Salmon Fishing On The Tweed*, first published in 1843, is still read for its curiosities. The

Grandtully ghost is a true story and happened when I was fishing from the Grandtully Hotel on Tayside at some time in the 1950s. The tanker driver on the Spey is again from a fishing-hut story about which I make the same proviso as before. The great salmon fisherman of the Spey was the late Sir Richard Levinge. The information about Alaska is mainly from the Alaskan Fishery and Game Department.

'Bosky Woods' takes sly digs at over-luxuriant writing about nature, superbly done by Evelyn Waugh in *Scoop*, which I've given as the Nature Notes approach; the angler-naturalist was David Jacques; and the final quotation about there being more to fishing than fishing comes from Howard Marshall (*Reflections On A River*, Witherby, 1969).

The essay about upstream wet-fly is irritating. I can't remember the river. My excuse is that I was young at the time. It might have been the Swale or the Ure or even the upper Hull just below Driffield Beck. It's impossible to say. My apologies. However, I can place the next story, about the hatch during a thunderstorm, with great precision: the West Dart about four hundred yards above Prince Hall. The French lake is Lou Pesquie, up in the Alps, inland from Cannes.

'Relations With Fish' starts with something true but puzzling: the grateful trout, if it was grateful, was taken and released on Beat 2 of the Arundel Arms water of the Lyd in Devon. The comment about Wimbleball was in a letter to the *Trout and Salmon* magazine. 'Arteful sport' was of course Berners; the American fisherman was Theodore Gordon, and monsters of the lake was a story told to me not long before he died by Lawrie Williamson of Blagdon. The argument about cruelty in fishing took place on television with a clergyman who was a member of the RSPCA, and undoubtedly a martyr to his cause. His name I have unfortunately mislaid.

'Bright Waters' begins with a true story about my wife and me in the car park just outside Usk on the Abergavenny road. We were fishing the town water and what a day it was. The flies that hatched quickly were on the Bolton Abbey beats of the Wharfe and those that hatched slowly were on the Abbots Barton water of the Itchen above Winchester. The evening rise came mainly from experiences at Leckford and Timsbury on the Test, the man in the red shirt was at Timsbury, and the story about London's rivers was by David Martin in the *Fly Fishers' Centenary Book*. The nice American was John Randolph, editor of *Fly Fisherman*. Jed Water near Jedburgh is located fairly well by the description in the text.

'A Touch Of Magic' is a favourite of mine, I can't really say why, except that there is a good deal of magic, to me at any rate, in Blagdon. I am grateful to Fred Buller for the 1905 cutting from *The Field* on catches, and to Tony Witherby for allowing me to quote Plunket Greene's description of Blagdon from *Where The Bright Waters Meet* (first edition, 1924; Witherby edition, 1969).

'Volcano Tea' celebrates two trips abroad, one to Ireland, the other to the United States. It was really my wife's trip to the United States as she was on a lecture tour, and exhausting it was, but we did have a day or so free, saw some wonderful rivers, met some wonderful people, and came back longing to go again. The same with Ireland, though Ireland was entirely a fishing holiday, without any other commitments. We stayed at the Newport House Hotel, Co. Mayo, and the loughs we fished were Beltra and Furnace and the river was the Newport river. If you want to get the flavour of Irish fishing there is nothing better than to read *A Man May Fish* by T. C. Kingsmill Moore (first edition 1960, second and revised edition, 1969, Colin Smythe Books) which contains, among other things, the brilliant portrait of Jamesie, the ghillie.

'Fly In The Sky' starts with one or two fishing hut stories and most of the rest of the chapter comes from some of my lecture notes, dolled up and made presentable. The piece about Dr Bell is based on something I wrote many years ago for *Trout and Salmon* magazine.

'Vice and Vises' is wonderful and I haven't done it justice. You could only deal with automated fly-tying and automated bait-fishing by quoting the advertisements in full, seeing them laid out in front of you, typeface, headlines, illustrations, the lot. Any summary of either vise or leurre is bound to be second best after that. I can't think how James Wright of Sprouston got mixed up in the same chapter but there he is and I've left him there.

The 'Sea Trout' chapter deals rather delicately with speculation about what happened to Mr Leavy's record fish after it had been worked over by the British Record (Rod Caught) Fish Committee in its rooms at Peterborough. In happier vein is the account of the right kind of preparation for a night's fishing – the river is the Lyd just above its junction with the Tamar. To fish the little burns that run down to the sea in the west of Scotland enquire at estate offices and the ironmonger's at Tarbert.

'Blue Grass' records some observations of nature which one comes across from time to time, mostly by accident. The blue grass quotation is from Ezra Pound. The eels which became blue grass were seen at Gunnislake weir fish-pass on the lower Tamar. The house by the Spey was Laggan House at Carron. The eagles were seen by rods fishing two boats on the Altnaharra Hotel water of Loch Hope in 1983. The remains of Achness village are at the junction of the Mallart and the Naver. The best book on the subject is John Prebble's *The Highland Clearances* (Secker and Warburg, 1963, also in Penguin) and there is a museum to the Clearances at Bettyhill. 'Love for the grannom' came from David Jacques (*Fisherman's Fly*, Black, 1965). The heron was fishing the river Lyd which flows past our cottage in Devon. For hawks and heronshaws consult Shakespeareans, such as Granville Barker, and others.

'Time Past Time' contains some fairly common reflections on time and words. *Truht* can be found in the reference books. The quotation is again Howard Marshall's, from the same book as before. The Wine Cellar pool is part of the Hungerford Town Water of the Kennet. The cottage garden invaded by badgers is our own at Lifton. The apartment block at Teddington was Thamespoint. A. E. Hobbs was the author of *Trout Of The Thames* (Herbert Jenkins, undated, probably around 1950) and a relative, H. A. van Zwanenberg, very kindly provided additional information and corrected some of my mistakes. The chalk-stream trout which savaged the flopping Caperer is of course from *A Summer On The Test* by J. Waller Hills (first edition, 1924, two subsequent editions, mine by Bles, 1946, and a paperback by Deutsch, 1985).

'Have You Seen My Husband' records an embarrassing encounter with a pretty lady, the wife of one of the rods at Two Lakes, near Romsey, which should be a lesson to us all. Tales from fishermen's huts were the source of the alligator story (much polished) and that of the mink.

'Hero Figures' came from brooding over a headline in *Trout Fisherman* magazine which said that someone, I can't remember who, was Britain's Number One Nymph Fisherman. It seemed worthy of interest. Bing Crosby's pipe was in a handout by the American Museum of Fly Fishing in Manchester, Vermont. The Lloyd George comment on Edward Grey came from a cutting.

'Literary Fishes' starts off with quotations from *Autobiography* by Neville Cardus, (Collins, 1947); then from *Rod and Line* by Arthur Ransome, (now in Oxford Paperback, 1980, originally published by Cape in 1929); from *Fly Fishing* by Viscount Grey of Fallodon, (enlarged edition, Dent, 1930, originally published in 1899); and lastly from *Bright Rivers*, by Nick Lyons, (Lippincott, Philadelphia and New York, 1977).